# LIVING A LEGACY THAT LASTS

*MARK CASELLA*

*with JENNY LUKEN*

*Foreword by John Affleck-Graves*

# LIVING A LEGACY THAT LASTS

Using the Success Mapping Process to Achieve What Matters Most to You and Your Family

 Third edition.
Printed in the United States of America

ISBN: 978-0-692-66940-2

Published by Coppertree, Ltd.
1101 St. Gregory Street, Suite 225
Cincinnati, Ohio 45202
513.579.1440
mark.casella@coppertreeltd.com
www.coppertreeltd.com

Designed by Scott Bruno, b graphic design

For information on bulk sales, scheduling Mark Casella as a speaker, or any of Coppertree's services please contact us at the email above.

# / CONTENTS /

Foreword.......vii
Preface.......xi
Acknowledgements.......xv
Introduction.......xix

**Part One: Getting to What Really Matters**

1 / Why Success Mapping?.......3

**Part Two: Guiding Your Today Through a Look at Your Yesterdays and Tomorrows**

2 / Mission: Articulating Your Family's Values.......13
3 / Family Mission and Your Legacy of Five.......25
4 / Vision: Defining the Well-Lived Life.......35

**Part Three: How to Use What You Have To Live a Legacy that Lasts**

5 / Boundaries Between the Family and the Enterprise.......51
6 / Governance: Making Family Decisions.......61
7 / Structuring the Vision: Priorities and Resources.......75
8 / The Legacy Strategy: Sustaining Success.......85

**Part Four: Challenges of Succession**

9 / Succession: Securing Your Future.......103
10 / Preparing and Positioning the Next Generation.......115
11 / Using Success Mapping to Manage Change.......125

**Part Five: Achieving Success**

12 / Executing the Legacy Strategy: Role of Advisors.......143

Onward!.......149

# Foreword

Each person is unique. We all have individual talents, characteristics, beliefs, and experiences that mold us into the person we are. While we may have some commonalities with others, no one is exactly the same as you. Similarly, each of our families is a unique blend of parents, siblings, uncles, aunts, and other relatives. Finally, the community in which we live is unique in terms of neighborhoods, businesses, amenities and natural beauty. Together these mold us into the distinctive individual we are and the way in which we perceive and experience our daily lives.

Because of this uniqueness, there is no one lifestyle that is right for everyone. There is no one solution to a problem, and there is no one way to plan for the future. This is the power and the beauty of Mark Casella's extraordinary book. It places our individuality at the forefront, while still providing a common blueprint each of us can follow to explore and nurture our distinctiveness, the uniqueness of our family situation, and the specifics of the community in which we live as we plan for the future and the legacy we will leave for future generations.

Early in his book, Mark challenges us to ask deep, but important questions. What do we want to leave as our legacy to future generations? How do we want them to remember us? Who and what is most important in our lives? No one can answer these questions but you. Importantly, as Mark forcibly reminds us, if you don't answer these questions for yourself, if you don't plan strategically and carefully, your legacy will happen by chance and circumstance. Like Tom in the very first chapter of the book, opportunity may be lost and your impact will be lessened.

Several years ago I had the privilege of working with the Confederated Salish and Kootenai Tribes in Northern Montana. We were faced with a difficult decision and one of the tribal elders admonished me to think of the seven generations that preceded us. What would they think of the decision we were taking? How would they judge us? It was a timely reminder that we are who we are because of those who preceded us. We are a product of the decisions they took, the sacrifices they made, and the opportunities they forged. It is they who laid the foundation of what we enjoy today and it is our responsibility to be true to that legacy.

The advice I received that day inspired me to think of my past, of the gifts I had been given by my parents. I came from a poor family so I did not have the gift of financial resources. However, from the earliest age I can remember, my father stressed the importance of education. Although not college educated himself, he insisted that I had that opportunity and both of my parents made enormous sacrifices so that I could attend college and then graduate school. It was their faith in education that transformed and enriched my life in ways they could not have imagined. It is this gift from them that made everything possible for me.

Like you, it is now my responsibility to provide the same opportunity for my family. That wise Salish and Kootenai tribal elder had more sage advice for me. In addition to considering how the prior seven generations would judge our decision, he invited us to consider how the succeeding seven generations would look back on the decision we were about to make. What will they think of us? How will our decision have influenced their beliefs, their character, and their lives? It is a sobering thought that, for better or for worse, the decisions you take today in planning for the future will impact the next seven generations. It may be a daunting concept, but you cannot avoid it!

Providing a lasting impact requires careful planning and this is the essence of this book. It lays out an easy, practical, but profound way, for you to plan your legacy. It recognizes your individuality and so provides a framework for you to create your unique solution, one that fits your character, your family, and your community. It recognizes that there are many aspects to your legacy. Yes, there is financial security and stability, but there is also much more. There are the values and ethical standards you uphold, the connectedness and stability of your family life, the love of those close to you, the strength and fellowship of the community in which you live.

Whether you are wealthy like Tom in the first chapter, or poor like my father, you have experiences, skills, values, and knowledge that you should pass on to succeeding generations. But, to maximize your impact, to protect those that you love most, and to provide transformative opportunities for future generations, takes careful strategic planning. It requires asking yourself the key questions raised in this book. At the evening of your life, what do you want as your legacy? What will you look back on as your most important contribution? How will you define success in your life? Only by following the guidance provided in this book, by planning as it suggests, will you truly be "living a legacy that lasts."

John Affleck-Graves, Ph.D
*Executive Vice President*
*The University of Notre Dame*

# Preface

"There's more to life than making money" is an accepted truism. I didn't always see life that way, though. Throughout my career as a financial advisor, I focused on making money for my clients and for myself. This is what I thought success meant to them. This is what I thought success meant to me.

Oddly, the more money my clients had, the less they wanted to talk about investing. It seemed my wealthiest clients were more interested in the success of their families, their communities, or their philanthropic pursuits. Of course, I was most interested in talking to them about how they would succeed by investing in my latest and greatest ideas. Why was making money so "unimportant" to them?

What was important? What did success mean to them? And what was it that kept them awake at night? This is what I wanted to understand. I wanted to help my clients and their families pursue what really mattered to them.

I was also waking up to something else. The people I wanted to talk to weren't all that interested in investing in the stock market in the first place. They were busy attending to their family enterprises. This is what they were invested in. This was their livelihood; it defined them. This was something they *did* want to talk about.

For 25 years, I'd provided private wealth management services as a financial advisor to individual investors. And during those 25 years I came to the realization that I wanted to be able to do more for the clients I served, especially those who owned an enterprise that was viewed as a multi-generational legacy asset for their families, such as a family business, vacation property, family foundation, or family office. And I wanted to be able to do more for my own family and the family business my father founded over 40 years ago.

If these people I admired and respected didn't want to talk about money, then neither did I. But what could I talk to them about? What did they want? How could I help them?

It was time for a change. I enrolled in Notre Dame's MBA program, left my job as a financial advisor, and in 2005 opened the doors of Coppertree, to help families focus on their journey and their legacy rather than their investments.

If success is more than just having a lot of money, then what is success? Success for families can mean many things. While contemporary American culture often equates success with winning, it's really much more. A life well lived could be the broadest measure of success. But what does a well-lived life look like? How do you live such a life?

So what does success mean to you? Like the families we serve, success for you is surely more than having a lot of money. What it is for you is what matters to me. If you ask most families what success means to them they will frequently mention ideals such as:

- Happiness and contentment for all family members
- Fulfillment for all family members in their life pursuits
- Connectedness to the family journey while supporting and celebrating each family member's unique life path
- Rewarding life experiences reflecting each family member's personal circumstances

This book was written to share what I've learned on my own journey. From my 35 years of professional experience and my personal perspective as a second-generation member of a business-owning family who's married to someone from the third generation of such a family, I'll show you what you can do to help your own family create a legacy that lasts.

This book will be a wake-up call for some. Sadly, we've seen amazingly successful family enterprises crash and burn because the owners didn't think they needed to do the hard work of planning for the future. Perhaps the lessons herein can change the outcome for families who haven't yet thoughtfully considered what needs to be done to be successful in pursuit of what matters most to them and to perpetuate their legacy for many generations.

What will your legacy say about you? Will your legacy last? Will you succeed in living a well lived life? If you are willing to invest the time and effort to use the success mapping process in your pursuit of what matters most to you and your family, then your prospects for the future are bright in living a lasting legacy.

# Acknowledgements

In the truest sense I should recognize every person I have ever met or encountered as all of them have contributed to me living a legacy that will last. As impractical as this would be, I am grateful to all the people in my life.

There are a number of special individuals who have touched me and inspired me that deserve my thanks.

First would be my family. Thank you Dad for being my role model, my mentor, and for believing in me every step of the way. Most especially thank you for all you did for me in helping to get Coppertree up and running. Mom, you made our family what it is today. You raised all of us with the love and devotion that helped to form who I am.

To Mike and Lynn, my brother and sister, my happy childhood memories are of the three of us as young children. I am also grateful for your love and support of me chasing my dream. Thanks to your families as well who have made me proud to say, I'm a Casella! Knowing that others believe in you makes it much easier to believe in yourself.

To my daughters, Katie, Sarah, Susan, and Grace, you too, believed in me and continually gave me words of encouragement as we worked to make Coppertree the success it is today. Now you have blessed us with beautiful families of your own. Woodrow, Jeff,

Patrick, and Patrick are just what I prayed for in son-in-laws. Now we turn to the future of our legacy as we delight in the addition of Hank, Taylor, Lila (and 2 more on the way!) as the next generation of the Casella Family Legacy.

I was blessed to marry into a great, loving, and spirit-filled family. I learned much about myself and grew in my faith through the love that I received from my wife's parents Ted and Ginny. Ted went to heaven in 2015 but not before he touched the lives of so many people, including me, in the humble work he did through organizations such as St. Vincent de Paul. Mom, you raised quite a family. Your legacy lives on in them.

As I began my journey that led to the creation of Coppertree, I was accepted into Notre Dame's MBA program in 2002. Each and every one of my classmates were an integral part of my growth experience there. I especially wish to thank Dr. John Affleck-Graves who continues to be a wonderful friend and supporter of the work we are doing for families across the country.

Special thanks to my ND study group—Jeff Heinichen, Mike Mathile, Jon McIntosh, Brian Smith, and Chris McLennan. I am glad that we continue to be friends many years later and am grateful for your help. Matt McConville was also in my study group and liked my idea so much that he became a member of the Coppertree team for a few short years to help me get up and running. Thanks Matt!

A very special thank you to another member of the ND family, Jim McGraw, who believed in Coppertree and me from the very first time he heard me talk about my ideas.

And to the families who have touched us and taught us, as well as those whom we have been honored to serve, thank you for the great work you are doing as a family and will continue to do for generations to come. Thanks to one of the very first families we served, Greg and Linda and your family, for your trust in us that we could make your life "simple." You are truly living a legacy that lasts.

This book came to life through the wise, thoughtful guidance and friendship of my editor, Howard Wells. I haven't had as much fun professionally for a long time as I had while writing this book with Howard. Your wit and expertise were the perfect combination in helping me bring this book to reality.

Finally, I want to thank my long-time business partner, Jenny Luken. Coppertree would not exist today without Jenny's involvement. She has skillfully guided the families we serve in gaining a better understanding of who they are and what they can do to flourish. Most importantly, she was there for me as a friend, a colleague and an equal regardless of the circumstances. Thank you good friend.

Last but not least, I am forever humbled by the love, support, encouragement and never-ending belief in me that Mary, my bride of 35 years, has given to me throughout our journey together and through all the ups and downs of bringing Coppertree to what it is today. I love you Mary!

# Introduction

What does success mean to you? What does it mean for your family?

Imagine that you're in the twilight of your life, surrounded by all the people, past and present, who are important to you. You're sharing the accomplishments you're most proud of. Someone asks you, "What about your family? What are you most proud of about your family?" How would you answer that question?

By what gauge would you measure your family's success? Money? Power? Contributions to the world? Or would it be something less tangible?

A Google search for the question "What does it mean to be family?" returned 954 million search results (hits). A search for "What is success?" returned 1.7 billion hits. A search for "How do you measure the success of your family?" yielded exactly *zero* responses. Apparently, no known methodologies exist for measuring the success of your family. Until now.

At Coppertree, we've developed tools that are making a big difference in the lives of the families we serve. The success mapping process in particular has tied all of our work together. It's the key to pursuing what matters most for families and individuals who understand the value of the journey itself.

Success mapping prompts you and your family to think about everything that matters to you, when you need to think about it. I want to help the people we work with to open their minds and really dream about *everything* that matters to them. So often, successful people are head down and dashing forward as fast as they can. Success mapping encourages them to *stop* ... and take a look at the world around them. What do they *really* want? What do *you* really want?

**How to Use This Book**

The stories in this book are based on the real experiences of families I've worked with over the course of my career, including my own. I've changed some details to protect my clients' privacy.

The book was written to share with you what I've learned. It also provides a how-to for anyone to use in living his or her own legacy in a meaningful way.

The book was written with two groups in mind.

The first is families and individuals who are interested in using the success mapping process as a guide for living a legacy that lasts. Whether families choose to utilize this process on their own or with the help of advisors, they can use this book to create and implement their legacy strategy in a holistic and integrated manner.

The second group is professional service providers. The success mapping process is a blueprint for service. While some of the process is already present in existing service models employed by professionals such as attorneys, accountants, financial advisors, bankers, and risk management advisors, the totality of the success mapping process can take the work of any advisor or advisory group to a higher level of service.

The book has five parts that will guide you through Coppertree's success mapping process.

Part One describes the kinds of issues that moved me to create the success mapping process through the story of Tom. I was one of Tom's financial advisors many years ago. Tom's saga will help you to understand why the success mapping process is so valuable to families and individuals.

Tom's legacy did not last. Now families like Tom's can realize a much different outcome through the use of the success mapping process.

Part Two and Part Three are the core of the book.

Part Two focuses on where the family has come from and where it wants to go. This is the Family Continuity Plan that includes:

- *Family Purpose:* What can you learn from your family's ancestral journey about yourself and your family? What makes your family unique? What are your family's values?
- *The influence of your Legacy of Five on Family Purpose:* Which family members have had the greatest impact on your life? What of your values and beliefs will have the most influence on your children and grandchildren?
- *Family Vision:* What does success mean to you and what does a well-lived life look like for you and your family? This is the heart of the success mapping process.

Part Three represents the nuts and bolts of the process for making decisions and establishing a plan to live a legacy that lasts including:

- *Boundaries:* Addresses the interplay between a family and its enterprise and the need for a decision-making structure to manage this interaction.
- *Family Governance:* How can families make decisions together around the issues they face? What rules and processes are needed to make good purpose-driven decisions?
- *Structuring the Vision:* How does the family prioritize their measures of success and what resources are needed to pursue what matters most to them?
- *Life Capital Framework and the Legacy Strategy:* How does the family sustain success using a strategic planning framework to pursue what they want to accomplish?

Part Four addresses the challenges of succession through two stories:

- *Ownership and Management Transition:* I share how my family has managed the change issues we faced as our family business transitioned through generations.
- *Family Education:* I also share my experiences with respect to my wife Mary's family businesses as an illustration of why education, transparency, and communication are vital to succession.
- *Managing Change:* This chapter offers guidance on how families can successfully manage change and conflict.

Part Five focuses on the role advisors can play in helping families with the execution of their legacy strategy.

Throughout the book, additional insight is also provided by my longtime business partner, Jenny Luken, who is a psychologist, family systems consultant and certified in the administration, interpretation and workshop facilitation of Myers-Briggs type indicator assessments. Jenny provides her expert viewpoint on many of the topics discussed in the book.

So what would you like to be able to say about your own family when you're looking back at your life and your journey?

This and many more questions are presented here to help you define what's important to you, what you want for yourself and your family, and how you can purposefully move forward in pursuing what matters most to you.

/ PART ONE /

# Getting to What Really Matters

# / 1 / Why Success Mapping?

Tom, a successful real estate developer, was one of my clients when I was a 30-something advisor working for a big investment firm. He had plenty invested in real estate, but very little in stocks and bonds. I went to great lengths to explain why he should move a portion of his wealth out of his real estate holdings and into a diversified portfolio I would carefully select for him.

But Tom was quite happy with his returns (they were exceeding 25 percent) and wasn't worried about the lack of diversity in his investments. He was now worth more than $100 million through this concentration in his real estate development company.

Then Tom took me by surprise. He said, "Mark, what I really want is for my kids to be happy in who they are and what they're doing. And I want them to want to be together as a family. All I see right now is that they're not getting along and don't seem to be happy with what's going on in their lives. That's what's on my mind."

Tom's oldest son lived on the West Coast with his wife and their three teenagers. Tom and his wife rarely got to be with them and missed seeing those grandkids growing up. Tom explained that his son had felt smothered when he lived in Cincinnati, where everyone knew him as "Tom's son." He wanted to be known for his own accomplishments rather than his father's. So he thought the best thing to do was to move away.

Next Tom talked about his daughter, who had moved to Florida when Tom's company wanted to take advantage of the real estate boom there. She had expressed an interest in joining Tom's business and this was his attempt to get her started.

Shortly after moving to Florida, she met up with the wrong crowd, who turned her on to the "joys" of cocaine. Tom eventually had to fire her because she was stealing money from the company to buy drugs. He was very worried about her and wanted her to come home to Cincinnati.

Tom's youngest son lived in Cincinnati with his wife and children. This son and his wife were both attorneys whose careers were thriving. Tom talked about how much he and his wife loved to spend time with this son, daughter-in-law, and "local" grandchildren. This was a bright spot in Tom's family life.

Even though they lived in different cities, Tom wanted the family to be close. He wished someone could help his family find a shared venture that would be a reason for them to want to come together.

I really wanted to be able to help him. But how? I was a financial advisor and didn't have the resources or the backing of my firm to address Tom's real needs.

At the time, I spoke only the language of investing. I didn't know how to talk to someone like Tom about the issues that were really on his mind. As a financial advisor, I couldn't help Tom help his children.

These kinds of conversations had played out on numerous occasions with other clients throughout my investment career. It was apparent to me that investing money was always down the list of priorities of what mattered most to the clients I served. And over time I realized that investing money for others was down my list of priorities as well.

**A Different Toolbox**

It was time for a change. The families I wanted to help needed a solution different from and complementary to what was being provided by a myriad of professional advisors.

What tools and resources would I need to help the Toms of the world? As the saying goes, if your only tool is a hammer, every problem looks like a nail. And that was my challenge. How could the hammer of wealth management help a family whose problem wasn't money but relationships?

And it wasn't just the use of my own toolbox that was at issue here. Most families' needs, I realized are at best partially served by any single advisor's toolbox. The financial advisor's toolbox addresses the solution in terms of investments. The attorney thinks of remedies based on legal agreements; the accountant presents tax-saving strategies as the answer. All of these are important, even essential. But none of them on their own can fully respond to the needs of a family trying to pursue what really matters most to them.

There had to be something else.

What I sensed was needed didn't exist. I would have to develop a new methodology that could help a family articulate what they really wanted and in turn craft a strategy that would bring together the family's existing advisors to produce an integrated, holistic response to the family's needs, wants, and aspirations.

I needed to create a new tool.

**Success Mapping Is Born**

As I started reading everything I could get my hands on, through Internet searches and trips to the library, I came across an article that highlighted a book written by Harvard professors Laura Nash and Howard Stevenson.

The authors conclude that success is much more than winning or being famous. They believe that "success is measured by the collection of activities that will be viewed affirmatively by you and those you care about—now, throughout your life, and beyond."[1]

Building on Nash and Stevenson's work, the success mapping process was created to help individuals and families identify what a well-lived life means to them and in turn determine the measureable activities they would want to pursue to achieve their vision of success.

The success mapping process prompts you to focus on four measures of success:

- How do I want to enjoy life?
- What goals have I set for myself?

1 Nash, Laura and Stevenson, Howard. *Just Enough: Tools for Creating Success in Your Work and Life.* Hoboken, New Jersey. John Wiley & Sons, 2004, 27

- How do I want to make a difference to those I care about?
- What of my values and beliefs do I want to pass on to those who follow after me?

Nash and Stevenson postulated that measuring success simply in terms of self, limits our ability to achieve what matters most. We also have a family life, a work life and one or more community interests and activities that we are a part of. Determining what success means within each of these dimensions—self, family, work, and community—would collectively articulate what a well lived life looks like.

While each of us is thinking about what we want for ourselves, we should also think about what we want as a family. Sometimes, our vision of personal success is the same as our vision of family success. Sometimes not. In both cases we need to understand the reason, the "why," that lies within each measure of success.

We also limit ourselves in thinking about what success can be by the self-imposed constraints we place in our lives. We all have limits but we also have possibilities. So, I ask questions about success from two perspectives. "What does it mean to you today based on your reality?" And "What would it look like in an unconstrained world?" We all look at life from our own perspective, blinkered by the limits we place on ourselves as well as the external ones we believe are beyond our capacity to overcome.

The tools of the success mapping process will help you live a legacy that lasts. Whether your circumstances find you very wealthy or you are of lesser means, this process provides the "what" that families can use in planning for the future. The success mapping process will give your family the ability to interpret and articulate what a well lived life means for you in your pursuit of what matters most and a framework for achieving your dreams.

**What Might Have Been**

Success mapping would have helped Tom and his family. Time and again in my career as a financial advisor, I witnessed families like Tom's fall apart because they didn't have a clear vision for the future. As the Cheshire Cat put it, "If you don't know where you're going, any road will take you there." Families who have a clear vision for the future are far more likely to be happy, fulfilled, and together.

Success mapping would have been helpful to Tom if he were thinking about his vast wealth being a resource for future generations. Our work has shown that when a wealth creator such as Tom shares his dreams for the family with his children, they understand his motivations for creating the wealth in the first place, and his expectations for how his wealth could be used to benefit them and their descendants.

Sadly, Tom did tell me what he wanted for his kids, but I doubt he ever told them. And this is the tragedy that befalls so many families. Without an understanding of what your dreams are for your family and yourself, decisions around family resources tend to be based on faulty assumptions.

By the time I was working with Tom, he had already transferred substantial sums into trusts for his children. Tom hated paying taxes, and this is what motivated him to transfer his money into these trusts. There was no consideration given to the impact these gifts would have on his children in the future.

The trusts also afforded Tom a veil of secrecy about his wealth. There was never any indication that his children knew what their father wanted of them and for them. Tom chose not to tell them what they were going to inherit someday, concerned that if they found out, their will to pursue their own careers would evaporate.

In fact, the kids were unaware that these trusts even existed until the eldest turned 30. Consequently, once the money started flowing to them it was like winning the lottery. They were ill prepared to manage their windfall. They had been set up to fail.

Did the attorney who devised the trusts realize that Tom worried his wealth would destroy his children? Maybe. Did the attorney know what Tom's dreams were for his family? Probably not. What could the attorney have learned about Tom through the success mapping process that could have produced a far more valuable mechanism for transferring Tom's wealth along with his values? Plenty.

The attorney would have learned that Tom valued being in business with his brother and that this was something he wanted for his children. With this knowledge, a purpose-driven wealth transfer plan might have been developed to promote the kids working together. In this way Tom's concern about the potential of his wealth to destroy his kids would be turned into an opportunity for them to work together and, more important, to interact with the legacy wealth in a productive manner together.

If one of Tom's measures of success for his kids was that they work together, they would have had a better chance of succeeding if he'd told them why this was important to him. Starting with the "what" and the "why" greatly enhances a family's potential to realize their dreams.

At least two other factors contributed to the demise of this family. First, Tom was a successful entrepreneur. Establishing and expanding his enterprise involved many decisions that had an element of risk, and more often than not, he made these decisions on his own, without outside advice or counsel.

Having risky solo decisions pay off leads many entrepreneurs to believe they don't need any input from anyone else ever. This attitude can cause many entrepreneurs to become overconfident and isolated. Especially when it comes to family matters, they rarely seek advice and oftentimes even shun it when it's offered by family members or outside experts.

This was a big problem for Tom's children—he wouldn't ask for their input on family matters. His paternalism didn't give them a voice. They felt their opinion didn't matter.

The second factor is a cousin of paternalism: generational influences. An ancient proverb says that men resemble their times more than they do their fathers. In other words, we are a product of the world into which we are born. Tom was born in 1930. People of this generation, often referred to as the Silent Generation, are typically characterized by values such as duty, honor, country. When asked the basis for his decisions, Tom would reply, "It's the right thing to do." Don't question ... just do it!

Taking these two factors into consideration, it's easier to understand how Silent Generation entrepreneurs can be perceived by their children as distant and brusque. In reality, this characterization couldn't be farther from the truth for the families we have worked with at Coppertree.

When we ask senior family members to describe their life journey, they reveal the stories and historical events that have shaped them.

As they tell their stories, they begin to open up. We learn what's on their minds and in their hearts as they describe what they want for their families.

The barriers that can keep a family from communicating come down, allowing for deep, meaningful connections between and within generations. Relationships that seem superficial can be transformed into much more significant ones when we let others know who we really are. Having an appreciation for how each generation's place on the timeline colors the way they interact with the world and the family goes a long way in breaking down the barriers to loving relationships in families.

In the end, Tom's children never learned his dream for them. They were not given the tools to keep them together. They are scattered across the country and show little interest in being together.

Tom's kids did learn how to be secretive and closed-minded from their father. His sons don't talk to their own families about money, much less their dreams. His daughter continues to struggle with her addiction and has broken off all communication with her brothers.

As I think back on Tom's quest to keep his family together the tools of the success mapping process could have given him and his family another way to plan for the future. They could have determined how best to use their resources to pursue what mattered most to them. They would have also been able to use this vision of what they wanted their future to look like as a guide for the various advisors and experts serving their family.

Tom and his wife died within a few years of each other. Their interest in the real estate business was sold to his brother's family and the proceeds were distributed to the children's trusts. Everything that Tom feared came to pass. The legacy he dreamt of did not survive the transition to his children's generation.

In a sense, Tom's dream of keeping his family together now lives on in me and the work I do for other families. Although I was unable to help him, the many conversations I had with him contributed to the founding of Coppertree. I'm now helping families like Tom's define and articulate what they want so they can thrive as a family and perpetuate their chosen legacy for generations.

**What This Means For You**

Creating and nurturing a multi-generational family legacy takes work. It's a process that focuses on purpose and vision, on open communication from everyone in the family, in a spirit of trust and a willingness to be vulnerable in sharing what matters most. Loving multi-generational families don't just happen. They make it happen for themselves today and in each subsequent generation.

What are you willing to do for your family? Are you willing to develop a plan based on purpose and vision? Are you willing to develop good communication skills that foster trust and respect? Are you willing to ensure that everyone in the family has the necessary tools and education to be positioned and prepared for the future?

/ PART TWO /

# Guiding Your Today Through a Look at Your Yesterdays and Your Tomorrows

/ 2 /

# Mission

## ARTICULATING YOUR FAMILY'S VALUES

What do you know about your family? What is your story? Why is this important?

Success mapping is a values-based understanding of who you and your family are and what you care about. You didn't just spring into existence today. You've come from somewhere, and that somewhere says a lot about who you are.

And so success mapping begins with a conversation about your family story. As the story unfolds, it reveals patterns, values, and experiences that influenced you and your family. The farther back you go, the more you'll learn about why you all are who you are today.

The Nelson family is a case in point.

### From Shopkeeping to Rocket Science

Carl and Victoria Nelson were introduced to Coppertree to help their family address succession planning. Carl started CVN Manufacturing over 40 years ago. He was now 70, she 68.

During my initial telephone conversation with Carl I learned their five adult children were not interested in working at CVN. He was struggling with what he should do with his company. Should he sell it since none of his family wanted to run it? Or should he explore other options on behalf of the family?

I explained the importance of framing these questions in the context of the family's values and beliefs to help him discern the "why" behind the decisions to be made. I also told him this would lead to the creation of their family's mission statement that could be used for decisions the family would face in the future. He liked this and arranged a time to meet with Coppertree.

During our initial meetings, Jenny Luken and I encourage our clients to share their story. We want to hear as much as they can tell us about themselves and what they know of their ancestry.

At our first meeting with a couple, we like to begin by asking how they first met as an ice-breaker. "How did you meet?" gets a big smile as a response followed by a walk down Memory Lane. The Nelson's were no different as they described how they met at a bar in college. They also described their courtship and other college experiences.

The Nelson's went on to tell us about the adjustments they had to make in the early days of their marriage as they settled in to a life together. They both expressed their gratitude for their parents' example of building a marriage on trust, flexibility, respect, and mutual support.

Both Carl and Victoria mentioned how important education was to them. They came from families who viewed education as the key to success. The couple also talked about how much they treasured family and how each of their families had established many traditions over the years to keep them together. Carl and Victoria certainly seemed to have compatible values.

We also asked them about the lives, experiences, and relationships of their families and to offer their thoughts on what these events meant to them.

Carl's family had been in the United States since the late 1800s. The generations followed a similar pattern. The men started and owned small businesses and the women raised children. Most of the businesses were nothing more than self-paying jobs—butcher shops and corner grocery stores.

As Carl talked about his ancestors, he realized there were a number of his relatives who were shopkeepers. He talked about his father and grandfather's belief that the women in their family should not work outside the home. Carl stated that he and Victoria didn't want their daughters to be constrained by this mind-set. They wanted their daughters and sons to pursue their dreams, wherever that might lead them.

Carl wondered why no one in his father's family had the ambition to grow their business beyond it being a paycheck. Fortunately, he noted that he learned to think of owning a business in a different way because of what Victoria's father did. He started a business from nothing and turned it into a large corporation.

Carl reiterated what he said during our initial phone conversation that none of their children had expressed an interest in succeeding him as the next leader of the business. He expressed his frustration that he would have to sell the business since none of the kids wanted to run the company. Carl thought the company's future was bright and that his kids had a lot to gain if he could find a successor to run the company after he retired.

Victoria's family journey was similar in some ways to that of Carl's family. Her father immigrated to the United States with his parents in the early 1900s from southern Europe in pursuit of the American dream, arriving with only the clothes on his back.

Victoria's father knew no one and had no specific idea of what he would do for a living other than he wanted to own his own business someday. This, he believed, would allow him to provide for his family and would be something he could pass on to his children.

Victoria's father went to work in the Pittsburgh steel mills shortly after arriving in this country. She said that her dad loved being a part of big industry. He wanted to understand how the steel barons of the last century grew so large. Many of them had also migrated from Europe.

Victoria's father saw that the auto industry was in the early stages of mass production and he wanted to find a way to get involved. He learned that while most of the parts that went into a car were made by the big auto companies, some car parts were made by other suppliers. This was his opportunity.

Victoria's father used all of his savings to buy a machine to make car parts. The business just took off from there. He was always on the lookout for more ways to supply the auto companies. She recalled how he once said that his biggest hurdle was he only had 24 hours a day.

Victoria's dad succeeded in achieving his American dream. He grew the business into a big corporation out of almost nothing. He was able to provide well for his family. She also remembered him talking about how he hoped the business would continue to provide for their family for a long time. He said that he very much wanted the business to be passed on to his kids and maybe even his grandkids.

Victoria's dad made it clear that only the boys could succeed him in running the business—this wasn't a business for girls. This attitude turned out to be a problem.

Victoria and her brothers had it good. They grew up wanting for nothing. They were too young to remember the early days of the business. All they experienced were the good times. Victoria appreciated that it was her dad's hard work and smarts that made his company so successful. Her brothers, Rob and Drew, just assumed they already had what it took to run the company. It didn't occur to them that it was their father's keen eye for making smart business decisions plus a lot of hard work that made his company so successful. Not only would they need to show up, they would also need to work as hard and as wisely as their dad did.

Victoria knew that her dad was concerned about her brothers. She could tell he wasn't sure they'd be able to run the company. But the old-world tradition of men working and women staying at home was too powerful for him to overcome. And so he put them in sales positions where he thought they could start to learn about the business. They learned plenty, but not about the business. They learned how to entertain customers a little too well. They both became very heavy drinkers. Eventually they both became alcoholics.

Victoria became aware that they didn't have the interests of the company's employees as their number one priority. Her dad always put the employees first. Employees were an extension of family in her dad's mind. He just assumed that Rob and Drew would treat the employees in the same manner. But that didn't turn out to be the case. The boys only thought about themselves.

Victoria saw that her dad learned how to manage the business as he grew the business. When he turned it over to her brothers, it was a big corporation. It required a much more sophisticated expertise to run than either of them had when they took it over. Neither of them bothered to learn the business. They were more interested in going to the bar.

Victoria described how Rob and Drew's ineptitude and alcoholism resulted in the business eventually being sold to a large automotive supplier in the early 1970s. They'd managed to turn a large, successful business into a shadow of its former glory.

Victoria and her brothers each got their share of the proceeds. She and Carl used the money to start CVN. Her brothers are destitute, divorced, and no longer a part of the family. She said that she certainly didn't want this to happen to her children.

What really saddened Victoria was that she wasn't given the opportunity to join the business because of her father's old-school mindset. At least he was fair and equal about ownership shares. She was pretty sure that had she been allowed to join the business as a manager, the outcome most likely would have been very different for her family because of her business school background.

I asked her what her father's feelings were about her going to business school. She told us that he was only interested in her going to a good school in the hopes of finding a worthy mate. He didn't care what she studied as long as she found a man. She told us that she was glad that she did in fact meet Carl at college and that she was equally proud of her business degree.

She told us that her degree proved to be very useful for CVN in the early days. She served as the finance and business manager for the company while Carl focused on sales and manufacturing. As the business grew she decided to retire so she could focus on raising their children. She reengaged with the company by joining its board once the kids had gone off to college.

Then I asked Carl and Victoria to tell us the story of CVN Manufacturing. Following completion of his graduate and undergraduate studies in aeronautical engineering Carl went to work for a large aerospace manufacturing company. Five years and several promotions later he left to start his own business.

CVN quickly established itself as a cutting-edge solution provider to the aerospace industry. The company positioned itself as partners with their customers rather than as a commoditized vendor who simply made airplane parts.

Carl was also an early adopter of qualifying for assurance certifications that identified CVN as a high quality manufacturer. He saw this as a differentiator from his competitors. Although all aerospace manufacturers would eventually be required to attain these certifications, many were slow to adopt them until they were forced to. This proved to be an important decision as this further established CVN as an industry leader. Now, over 40 years later, CVN was recognized as a global leader in aerospace manufacturing.

Carl said that he saw the business as an important contributor to the success of the family. He also talked about the business's potential to be a resource for future generations of the family as long as each generation was realistic about their expectations of the company. In other words, the growth of the family and the growth of the business would determine what CVN could afford to distribute.

Carl and Victoria had shared their story with us in a way that allowed us to diagram their families in a family map known as a *genogram.*

A genogram (Figure 2.1) gives us the ability to organize large amounts of information about a family, helping us see patterns of activity, behavior, and attitudes that are transmitted across generations. It's a combination of genealogical information, such as births, deaths, marriages, and separations, and a timeline of important life events. We're looking for clues to the values, beliefs, and behaviors that have formed this family.

Once completed, the genogram is a powerful depiction of a family's life story. We have witnessed many a-ha moments as family members study the genogram and begin to realize which events and patterns have shaped their own lives.

---

**Jenny's View: What the Genogram Reveals**

The family into which we are born is known as our family of origin. That environment becomes our frame of reference for all that we know, at least until we are physically equipped to move into the outside world.

We are who we are because of those who have come before us. We didn't acquire our behaviors, habits, temperaments, and genetic tendencies in a vacuum. We are a product of the past and present generations of our family.

When we use the genogram, we're looking at the family as an interlocking system where each generation, household, or individual has

**Figure 2.1 / Carl and Victoria Nelson Ancestral Genogram**

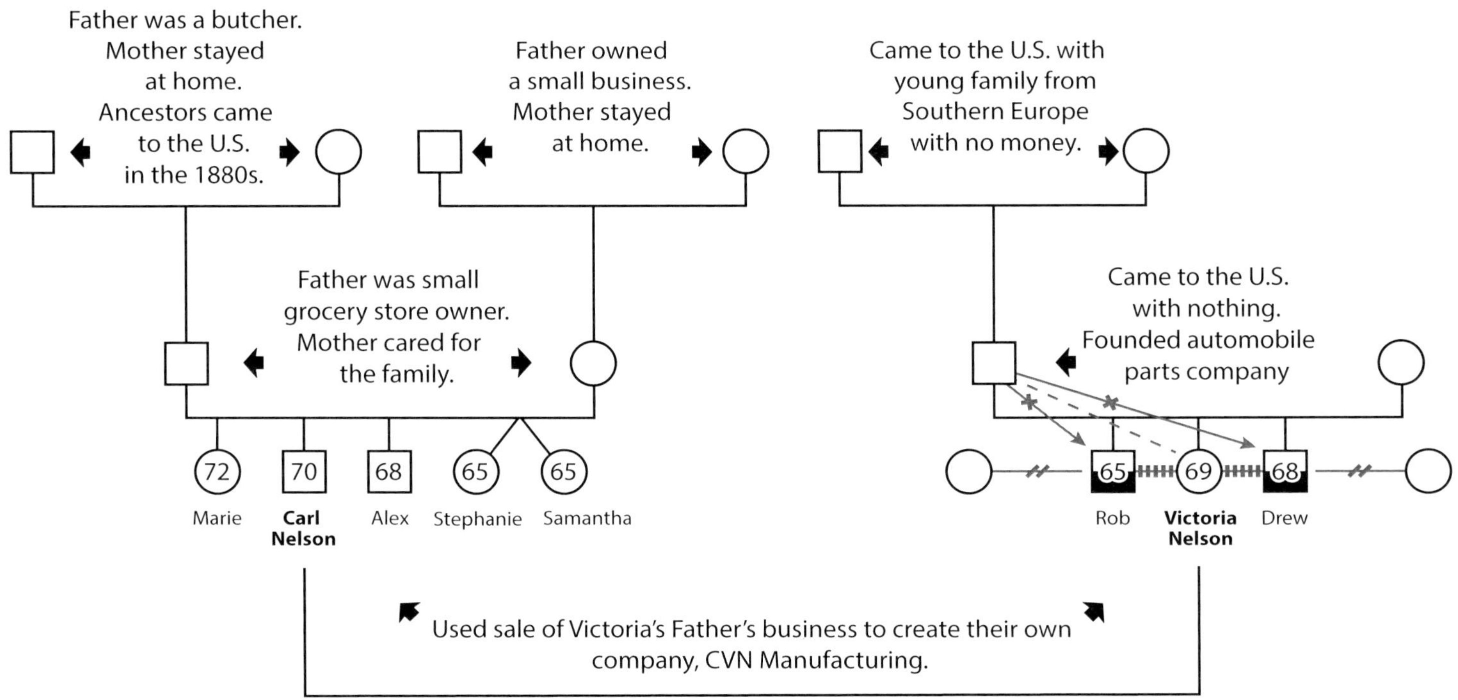

an effect on the others, especially in times of change, stress, or conflict. Looking at all the components of that system provides a broader context of what is influencing the family than just looking at one person or one issue.

More than a detailed version of a family tree, a genogram is a tool that is widely used by medical practitioners and family therapists to organize a person's family history. In our practice, this family diagram is a rich source of information for us and our clients.

A genogram allows us to identify life events that can cause stress or anxiety in a family. It can also identify relationship patterns that have been in play for generations and are working their way through the family. It illustrates the power of the family dynamic to shape the family. For families who own businesses, this dynamic may affect their enterprise as well.

What at first seems a confusing jumble of circles, squares, and squiggly lines tells the story of the family's journey. This may include the tale of the immigrant journey from overseas and how the family established itself once here. The genogram may also uncover relationships that may have been strained or broken as well as those that were strong and sustaining.

When family members start talking about the stories behind each of the circles (women) and squares (men), they begin to open up about the true fabric of the family. We frequently hear phrases like "I never realized what effect my aunt and uncle's divorce had on my cousins" or "I'm not really sure why we don't talk to Aunt Nancy's kids. I think she and Mom had a big fight, but I miss them."

This can open their minds to the idea that they may be repeating or avoiding patterns in their family system but, more important, by looking at their family in this way they have an opportunity to choose what they want their relationship lines to look like.

Family systems theory, pioneered by psychologist Murray Bowen in the 1960s, underlines the importance of understanding how each of us is a part of something bigger than ourselves. It can also give us insight into how we relate to others outside our immediate family.

### The Family Story = The Family Values

When we begin the genogram process, participating family members usually approach it as a basic accounting of relatives they knew personally. They're also recalling stories about how family members reared their children and reacted to adversity. Many families have supported their children through college because education is something they value. Many families overcame obstacles as they were establishing their business through hard work and perseverance, also values the family embraced.

In recognizing the values that come through in their story, family members can begin to determine which values are truly important to them and how they wish to live them. What does prioritizing education look like? What does having family support as a value look like in real life? These are the questions families begin to address as they discover and articulate their values.

**Celebrating Family Traditions**

The genogram process helps individuals memorialize their family story for their children and generations to come. Through the process, we uncover traditions that may have not been articulated as such, but have become an important thread in the fabric of the family.

The process helps them understand and appreciate how their history has formed them into who they are today. As we go through this exercise with a family, they may be describing the traditions of a beloved aunt's holiday parties or Sunday visits to their grandfather's house and suddenly realize the impact that person has had on them and/or the family.

As family traditions are passed on from one generation to the next, so too are the values embodied in them. Carrying on these traditions can deepen relationships and promote emotional closeness within the family. As the family grows, honoring and celebrating the family's traditions become ever more important in keeping the family together.

For families who collectively own and benefit from a family business, the genogram process can help strengthen relationships within the family through their increased awareness of how the enterprise touched their lives and helped shape the family over time. If the family can maintain a connection to their purpose as defined by their values and traditions, they are more likely to continue to benefit from their enterprise through the third, fourth, and in some cases the fifth generation.

**The Timeline: External Influences**

While family members are recounting the lives of those who have come before them, we're also paying attention to what was going on in the world at various points in the family's history. For example, World War II was a big influence in many of our clients' lives. Women went to work and/or became widows while men went off to war. Many veterans came home after the war to start their families and businesses, giving us the Baby Boom and decades of economic prosperity throughout the nation.

The cultural effect of the outside world can be a significant influence, as families adjust their lives to meet different challenges such as war, recession, or even Prohibition. We have seen these various types of societal events turn out to be major factors in shaping our clients' lives. Taking into consideration the impact of external factors on a family's journey allows the family to understand why things may or may not have happened the way they did.

Carl and Victoria learned much more from their family stories as we walked them through the genogram process. The experiences and relationships they shared with us were key to understanding what was and is important to their family.

The next step in this process was to go through a similar exercise with each of their children and spouses by household. Our objective throughout was to identify the values and beliefs that would define what mattered most to the Nelson family. The family's values form the basis for the creation of a family mission statement.

**The Family Mission Statement**

We brought the adult members of the Nelson family together in a meeting to create their family mission statement. This statement clarifies the "why" or purpose that drives the family forward and grows naturally out of the values we helped them recognize.

Carl and Victoria's family identified the following values and beliefs to be included in the mission statement:

- Achievement: A sense of accomplishment, success or contribution
- Competitiveness : Taking risks, winning
- Courage: Standing up for your beliefs
- Equality: Respecting everyone's rights
- Family: Taking care of and spending time with loved ones
- Freedom: Embracing liberty; exercising free will
- Tradition: Respecting an established way of doing things
- Integrity: Honesty, sincerity, genuineness
- Leadership: Guiding people and projects; setting the pace

- Opportunity: Having the chance to experience progress and advancement
- Personal growth: Pursuing new skills and self-awareness
- Personal responsibility: Voluntarily doing what is expected of you
- Risk: Exploring the unknown; testing limits
- Spiritual growth: Deepening our relationship with our Creator
- Innovation: Finding new and creative ways of doing things

These values were synthesized into their family mission statement:

---

**The Carl & Victoria Nelson Family Mission Statement**
We, the Nelson Family, pledge to pursue our vision for our family's future with discipline, focus, patience, honesty, and understanding, as well as a passion for working with all members of our family.

*To accomplish this, our family will:*

- Acknowledge, honor, and respect the hard work, history, love, and legacy of our family's earlier generations. Our family founder's dream is that the family's enterprise wealth would last a long time and be used in ways that would benefit not just present generations, but also society, and future generations of our family yet to come.
- Remain united through our heritage, maintain positive family relations, communicate effectively, and promote decision-making structures which assure the success of those to follow.
- Accept our good fortune as a resource for empowering each family member to become the best he or she can be, and willingly embrace our responsibility to give back.
- Develop the competencies to handle the responsibilities of wealth, effectively pursue the opportunities that come before us, and become caring and compassionate members of our community.

### What This Means For You

Understanding where you've come from is an important step in living your legacy. It provides the historic context of what you stand for. Your life journey and that of your family have helped form who you are. It gives meaning and purpose to how you make decisions.

What do you stand for? What do you believe? What of your values will others see as your legacy?

/ 3 /

# Family Mission and Your Legacy of Five

As you think about your family story, who had the most influence on who you are today?

During your life journey you will probably connect with five generations of your family: grandparents; parents, aunts, uncles; brothers, sisters, cousins, spouse; children, nieces, nephews; and grandchildren. These family members will have the greatest impact on who you are and what you contribute to your family legacy. And we each have our own personal legacy of self that has a role in how the family story plays out. We call these generational relationships your Legacy of Five.

The Legacy of Five rolls one generation forward as each new generation is born and joins the family. Through this process, the family legacy is changing and evolving as each generation's Legacy of Five unfolds.

Your family's legacy may also be defined by the ancestral generations that date back centuries. Those generations can be important factors to your family legacy. But none are more relevant to present generations of your family than those of the Legacy of Five. These are the generations that you were personally involved with throughout your life.

How do each of these Legacy of Five generations affect you and your family? It depends on where you are on your life journey—the story of you. It depends on whether you are receiving from or giving to your Legacy of Five.

The Legacy of Five gives us an understanding of what our family stands for, our mission. Then we in turn become the teacher as we pass on our values to our children and grandchildren. We each contribute to our Legacy of Five through our own values and beliefs that are unique to us.

Within my Legacy of Five, my grandfather Vito initially defined our family legacy by having the courage to pursue his dream. He wanted to provide a better life for his family than the life of poverty he experienced as a boy. Vito was the oldest of more than 20 children. (We don't know the total number of his siblings since he left Italy before his parents ceased having children.)

At the age of 24, he immigrated from Italy to the United States. He left his family and ventured halfway around the world all by himself to pursue the American Dream of being able to provide that better life for his family.

After passing through Ellis Island he stayed with friends of his parents who had come to the United States a few years earlier. They helped him find a job with the B&O Railroad. He soon met his wife, Bambina, who had emigrated to the U.S. with her father and mother. She was 10 years younger than Vito. Shortly thereafter Vito was promoted to a yard foreman. The railroad moved him to Dayton, Ohio where they raised their six children and lived for the remainder of their lives. My grandfather lived to be 86 years old. I did not know my grandmother because she died when I was a baby.

My grandfather contributed to my Legacy of Five through his journey to America. He believed in pursuing his dreams, living in accordance with your faith and beliefs, hard work, perseverance and ambition. These values live on in me today.

His son, my father Frank, also valued having the courage to pursue his dream. He wanted to be his own boss. He gave up his job as a tool maker to start his own tool company. And he kept Grandpa's American Dream of providing a better life for our family alive. There were many more Legacy of Five family members whom I interacted with and received from that helped shaped who I've become today.

Grandpa's and Dad's dreams live on in me: I had the courage to leave a lucrative career in investment counseling to create my own company so I could pursue my dream of helping our family and other families perpetuate their legacy for multiple generations.

As Mary and I brought our four daughters into the world my Legacy of Five evolved. Now I was as much a giver of the legacy as I was a receiver in my younger days. Legacy is always about giving and receiving. We brought into our home the values and beliefs we received from our ancestral Legacies of Five. We gave our children the values of love, family, education, hard work, dedication, patience, perseverance, courage, faith, and unity.

The fifth generation of Mary's and my Legacy of Five is now a reality. We have three grandchildren and counting. Now in turn, we are the first generation of their Legacy of Five. Our dream for them is that they stay together, love one another and always put family first.

Can you have a connection to the family legacy beyond your Legacy of Five? Yes. This connection most often comes in the form of a family asset such as a family-owned business, resort property, or foundation, perhaps dating back generations. Because some family members may see this legacy resource as a burden that has been placed on them, connecting each generation to the family story is crucial.

Helping everyone understand and, ideally, appreciate what their ancestors had to do to be successful increases the potential for each new generation to be responsible stewards of the legacy for future generations. Legacy assets can very well be the bond that keeps a family together for many generations.

How will your Legacy of Five impact what your family stands for, both today and in the future? We all will leave a legacy. You have the power to decide what that legacy will be. What are you doing to shape your legacy?

The Miller family is a case in point.

### An Entrepreneurial Legacy of Five

George Miller became a financially successful entrepreneur late in life. After working for a large manufacturer of household products for most of his career, George was hired by a fast-growing consumer electronics company to be the VP of product development.

A private equity investor bought the company from the founders and promoted George to president. As an incentive, he was given an interest in the company for his sweat equity in running it. This proved to be a lucrative opportunity.

George quickly improved the company's financial performance. As a result of his efforts, the business was sold to another private equity group a few years later for a substantial profit. George had hit the jackpot. He used some of his proceeds to reinvest in the company alongside the new ownership group. He was asked to continue doing what he had done before, and lo and behold, the company was sold once again. His managerial genius had translated into another cash windfall.

George came to Coppertree because he was looking for help managing his family's affairs. We agreed to develop a legacy strategy that reflected what he wanted for himself and his family. We would also work with his other advisors to coordinate the myriad of transactions and activities necessary to meet his family's needs.

The first step was to get to know the Miller family. We wanted to hear their story and, specifically, about their Legacy of Five.

At our first meeting with George and his wife Lindsay, we asked them to tell us the story of their families. We learned that George was 58 and Lindsay was 53. Their son Peter was 24 and their daughter Michelle was 22.

We learned about their experiences with their grandparents, parents, aunts, and uncles. We also learned what their parents and grandparents told them about their earlier ancestors. Their ancestors each contributed in some way to the family legacy and helped form who George and Lindsay had become.

Lindsay's grandfather was an important influence on her Legacy of Five. He gave up his dream when he dropped out of medical school to take over their struggling family farm after his father had passed away. He told Lindsay that nothing was more important than family and that we needed to do everything we could to help each other out.

This Legacy of Five experience lived on in George and Lindsay as they wanted to help their son and daughter pursue their dreams.

Their ancestral generations had taught them that family resources were to be used for the good of the family during their lifetime rather than after they had passed on.

### The Family Meeting

During a subsequent family meeting, George and Lindsay told their kids that, as was tradition in their families, they would support them in pursuing their dreams by providing the financial resources they would need. Their son had been talking about starting a furniture company and their daughter had indicated she might want to go back to school.

George and Lindsay told Peter and Michelle what their expectations were in sharing their wealth with them. George said he wanted them to be serious in their undertakings. Lindsay added that she wanted them to be committed and carry through to the end.

They went on to say that if their son wanted to start his own company, they wanted to see a business plan. If their daughter was going to embark on a new field of study, they expected her to complete the program and earn her degree.

We counseled George and Lindsay to fund significant ventures their kids wished to pursue by lending them money rather than giving it to them outright. In this way, as the ventures became successful, the kids could repay the "bank," thus replenishing the family's pool of legacy wealth.

We asked Peter and Michelle to talk about their dreams.

### The Legacy of Five Rolls On...

I asked Peter what was important to him about starting his own business. He said that he wanted to be a wealth creator in his own right. With that said, Peter then asked his parents if they were willing to help fund the start-up costs associated with launching his furniture company. They both said yes.

Peter believed he would pay his parents' investment in him forward to future generations. The influence of his parents' willingness to share their wealth with him became a part of his Legacy of Five.

Peter was also influenced by the time he had spent with his grandparents. His paternal grandmother was a schoolteacher for many years. He never forgot what he learned from her: "Education is the lifeblood of freedom and prosperity. Never squander an opportunity to learn more. This is important not only for you but for your family." She asked him to promise her that he would heed her advice and he did.

Peter married a few years later. The Millers' granddaughter, Carrie, was born the following year. Peter and his wife started planning for their daughter's education as soon as she was born. Peter is fulfilling that Legacy of Five promise he made to his grandmother every time they add money to their daughter's education fund.

**...and On**

The Millers' daughter Michelle, who lived on the West Coast, was following in her mother's footsteps performing and choreographing shows for the local community theater as part of her own Legacy of Five. Following in her grandparents' footsteps, she told her parents that she could see herself enrolling in a doctoral program in the performing arts and eventually becoming a university professor as another contribution to the family legacy. George and Lindsay told her they would gladly pay the expenses associated with her doctoral studies.

Michelle married recently and is now working her way through her doctoral program in California. Her husband is exploring business ventures. The Millers said they'd help him if he needed money to pursue one.

Michelle also learned from her parents that each new generation should work to replenish and expand the family's resources to help their children and future generations find their own success in life. To her, this meant that each generation needed to contribute to the family legacy through wealth-creating ventures, whether owning a business like her brother's or hiring financial advisors to select wealth-creating investments on her behalf.

Michelle and her husband chose to contribute to the legacy by overseeing the family's financial assets as passive investors. As such, they have agreed to serve on the family investment committee where they are involved with supervising and evaluating the family's financial advisors to ensure they are meeting the family's expectations and fulfilling their needs. This is another way they contributed to the family legacy based on their Legacy of Five experiences.

**Tying It All Together**

Each generation's Legacy of Five impacts the family legacy. George and Lindsay's Legacy of Five included the wise advice of Lindsay's grandfather to put family first and to do whatever you could to help your family thrive. That became a part of the family's legacy and values that would shape the family for generations.

The Millers' children, Peter and Michelle were influenced by their grandparents, who encouraged them to obtain the highest degree of education they could.

The personal experiences of your Legacy of Five and the legacy values that are passed on from previous generations form and shape who and what the family is today and who you are today.

The challenge for you as you give to your Legacy of Five, your family legacy, and your legacy of self, is to understand how you can shape your legacy. How will you know if you were successful? It starts by understanding what you define as success.

---

**Jenny's Perspective: What Happened Here?**

George and Lindsay took the time to communicate with their children about what most people think of as a difficult topic: money. It was no secret to Peter and Michelle that their parents had created financial wealth for themselves, but no one up to this point, had talked about what it meant for them, the children. It's not that they expected anything, they just didn't know.

In the Millers' case, their goal was to 'help our children achieve their dreams while we're still alive.'

This was something both George and Lindsay felt strongly about. They knew that when they died, their kids would be wealthy. Their desire was to have the family wealth benefit Peter and Michelle now so that Peter could start his furniture company and Michelle could continue her education. What they didn't want was for their children to open the mailbox one day, receive a big check, and not have it attached to what they wanted the money to mean.

What also happened, however, was a thoughtful and heartfelt conversation that affirmed this was not only financial, but emotional. This gift to their children was from their heart. Having this conversation gave all of them the chance to fully discuss and be clear about what the gift meant. They became part of a team, all on board to help each other achieve their goals.

For many families of wealth, especially those with multi-generational wealth, talking about how much, who gets what, and other topics surrounding money is considered tasteless and often avoided. These conversations are also hard for many people to initiate.

When parents begin these conversations by expressing their heartfelt hopes for their children rather than focusing on the family's financial wealth, the discussion becomes easier and more meaningful, unencumbered by things that sometimes get in the way of the best intentions.

What happens when an individual learns of their inheritance through the reading of a will? As a legal document, wills usually describes the amount, but not the intent of the benefactor. That is a lost opportunity to put meaning into why the gift was made. In this case, heirs are usually left with no idea of what their parents wanted for them.

One of the most frequent reasons Coppertree is called on is to help the family, the giver and the receiver, sort out what the gift means. At this point, the family has recognized that a financial gift, without explanation as to what it means, has or will soon become a burden to the receiver.

Something we hear often is, "I don't want this money to ruin my kids, and I don't want the kids to feel entitled to the point that they never find their own passion." Or lurking just below the surface is the idea that the parents usually want their children to be self-supporting beyond what they will inherit or have already been given. Self-confidence, personal responsibility, and the great joy of learning from failing and eventually succeeding are all things a trust fund or a large financial gift cannot buy.

The true gift is when the giver has taken the time to have a thoughtful conversation with the recipient(s) that includes:

- This is what we are gifting to you but, more important, this is why.
- This is what you can expect from us and this is what we expect from you.
- We will all work on making this succeed and here is the plan.

**What This Means For You**

From grandparents to grandkids, this is the span of generations that will most likely influence who you are and what your version of the family legacy means to you. These are also the generations who will be most impacted by you.

Your family's legacy may span beyond your Legacy of Five. It may include older generations and it may last well into many future generations. Your Legacy of Five and your family legacy may be similar or quite different. Both may have an impact on who you are.

Who's impacted your legacy? Whose legacy will you impact?

/ 4 /

# Vision

## DEFINING THE WELL-LIVED LIFE

It's the journey that matters. Where you end up is of little significance if you didn't take time to live in each and every moment. True success in life is measured more by the quality of your journey and what you do on your journey than by reaching your eventual destination.

What does a journey, filled with successes mean to you, and what does a well-lived life look like for you and your family? This vision for your life is the core of the success mapping process.

The Dawson family is a case in point.

### A New Vision for the Dawson Family

Following a brief stint as a computer sciences professor at a Boston-area university, Kevin Dawson decided to start his own data analytics company in Greenwich, Connecticut. Ten years later, the business had grown considerably and several private equity firms convinced Kevin to sell the majority of his business to them. His personal wealth was now in the hundreds of millions of dollars.

Kevin and his wife Christy were caught off guard by their sudden wealth. They didn't come from money—their parents were solidly middle-class white-collar professionals who valued education, personal responsibility, and family life.

Kevin and Christy lived their parents' values. They both attended top-notch universities and following graduation got married, started a family, and worked hard to get to where they were now. Their twin boys were now 16.

Kevin's enormous financial successes put the family on a different path than his parents'. The Dawsons bought a beautiful estate in Greenwich. Their boys were enrolled in the most prestigious private school in Connecticut and beginning to think about college. And Christy was finding her own successes in a business she had started two years earlier.

Everyone in the family seemed to be in a good place, but something was bothering Kevin. He worried about how the boys would be affected by the wealth he had created. Talking to friends and colleagues who were also wealthy, he realized he wasn't alone in his concerns.

Kevin and Christy agreed they needed to help the boys find their own paths in life without the money destroying their will to pursue what they wanted for themselves. Like many of their friends, they believed it might be best to give their fortune to charity rather than risking the adverse effects that inheriting substantial wealth might have on the boys.

The Dawsons arranged a meeting with their family attorney to discuss this idea. Christy asked their attorney what he thought about setting up a foundation so they could give most of their money away rather than bequeathing it to their sons. She told him they wanted to give some money to the boys, but not enough that they could afford to do nothing with their lives.

Their attorney responded that families of wealth have a great privilege and responsibility to use their resources to make the world a better place. He went on to say that families of substantial wealth rarely spend all that they have created or inherited.

Their attorney asked whether they had ever thought of their wealth as being a force for good for their sons. They said no. All they could think about was how dangerous it might be for their sons to be given so much money. He asked them what they wanted most for their boys.

They said they wanted their boys to be happy, and to have meaningful and productive careers. Their attorney asked them what yardstick they believed accurately measured success. The Dawsons said doing something that made you happy and fulfilled was a better measure of success than simply making a lot of money.

The Dawsons attorney wanted to know whether they thought having enough money to do what you want was important. They nodded and said money certainly made it easier to do some things in life. But they didn't want their money to rob the boys of their own ambitions.

Their attorney asked how they would feel if the boys wanted to pursue careers in fields such as social work or the nonprofit sector. Kevin and Christy both stated they didn't care how much money the boys made as long as the work they were doing was important to them.

He asked them how they felt about the boys not being able to do some of the things they'd always enjoyed doing as a family, like skiing in the Alps every other winter. He explained the obvious. As social workers or nonprofit administrators, the boys wouldn't be able to afford such vacations. If Kevin and Christy opted to give all their money to charity, how would their sons continue to enjoy the quality of life they were accustomed to?

Before the Dawsons could answer, their attorney introduced the thought that money itself wasn't destructive should they choose to share their vast wealth with the boys. To avert a sense of entitlement, he said, they would need to educate their sons on how to interact with their wealth in a good way. The attorney also emphasized the importance of clarifying for the boys what the family stood for and how this money could be used as a resource to perpetuate the family legacy through them and eventually their own families.

All of these considerations were addressed through the success mapping process.

**A Vision of Fulfillment**

The Dawsons' attorney introduced them to Coppertree to go through the success mapping process. The process showed the Dawsons how their wealth could be used to pursue what mattered most to them. The Dawsons also gained clarity on what they wanted for their boys. The money itself became less of a worry. Now their focus was more about helping their sons follow their dreams.

The success mapping process also gave them the tools to educate their sons to be stewards of the family's wealth. The Dawsons realized their assets were large enough to be a resource for current generations of their family. The Dawson boys and future generations of the family, however, would be expected to contribute to the growth of the family's wealth in support of an ever-growing number of family members.

In the end, the Dawsons changed their minds about giving all their money to charity and chose to make most of it available to the family. Their sons would receive distributions as they reached certain milestones. The Dawsons also created a family foundation that they as a family would direct, making grants that would reflect the family's values.

The Dawsons were now focused on the journey they lived each day. They were relieved once they had a vision for their future and a plan to pursue what they wanted for themselves and their sons. They now think about the boys' future in a positive way, rather than worrying about how the money might destroy them.

Through the success mapping process Kevin and Christy learned their sons were interested in working with mentally disabled children—their cousin Wendy was diagnosed with autism shortly after birth. They became very close with their cousin and went to summer camp with her each year. The Dawson boys loved seeing how all of the kids enjoyed their time at camp.

In the ensuing year, as Kevin and Christy encouraged the boys to dream about things they wanted to do, they both talked about wanting to start their own camp for children with special needs. The whole family went to work on this dream immediately. Camp Wendy is now up and running and making a big difference in the lives of many families who have children with special needs.

### Articulating Your Vision of Success

The success mapping process gives you the ability to fully articulate your vision of what a well-lived life means to you. Simply put, it will help you determine where you want to go with your life. The goals and aspirations you identify through success mapping give you clarity on your direction. Ask yourself these questions:

What do I want for myself, my family, my work, my community in terms of:

- Enjoyment and happiness?
- Accomplishments?
- Making a difference?
- Values, beliefs and legacy?[2]

## The Vision Interview

The vision interview guide (figure 4.1) depicts the process as a grid that addresses the four dimensions of success. Within each dimension, the four measures of success are explored. Each dimension and each metric can have any number of considerations or interests associated with it.

The first step in completing this grid is to identify what you personally envision as a well-lived life for yourself with respect to each of the measures. The first metric asks you how you want to enjoy life personally. In the interview, we would explore what you enjoy doing now, what you've enjoyed in the past, and what you think you'd enjoy in the future.

If we were interviewing you, as we did with Carl and Victoria Nelson, we'd ask you first to describe what you do for enjoyment, then what you'd do if you had unlimited resources. If you can truly ignore boundaries and constraints, this can be a very freeing exercise.

Everything that comes to mind with respect to how you want to personally enjoy life is added to this box. As you might expect, this list of ideas for what makes you happy may become quite lengthy. That's okay. The goal here is to envision how you want to enjoy life, with no limits on your imagination.

In the next box in the column you'd list the accomplishments you want to achieve in your lifetime. Throughout this exercise quantity of ideas as well as quality is important.

The final two boxes in the column are addressed in a similar manner.

Sometimes, you may find nothing to include for one of the measures within a dimension. There is no need to make something up; just leave it blank.

Once the process is completed, all of the measures for what matters most across the four dimensions are compiled into a single list.

---

2 Based on Laura Nash and Howard Stevenson, *Just Enough: Tools for Creating Success in Your Work and Life* (Hoboken, N.J.: Wiley, 2004), p. 100.

**Figure 4.1 / Vision Interview Guide**

| | SELF | FAMILY | ENTERPRISE | COMMUNITY |
|---|---|---|---|---|
| | *Determining My Expectations for Living A Well-Lived Life* | *Determining Our Expectations for Living A Well-Lived Life* | *Determining Our Expectations of Our Enterprise* | *Determining Our Expectations As Members of Our Community* |
| HAPPINESS | **Enjoying Life** How do I wish to enjoy life personally? | **Family Enjoyment** How do we wish to enjoy life as a family? | **Supporting the Family** How can our Enterprise support the family in a positive, energetic, and respectful environment? | **Community Activities** What community activities do we want to be involved with that are enjoyable? |
| ACHIEVEMENT | **Goals/Accomplishments** What do I want to accomplish during my lifetime? | **Family Goals** What do we intend to accomplish as a family? | **Enterprise Goals** What do we want of our Enterprise? | **Good Citizenry** What can we do to be good citizens of our communities? |
| SIGNIFICANCE | **Making a Difference** What can I do to impact the people I care about? | **Family Impact** What can our family do to impact present and future generations of our family? | **Stakeholder Impact** How can our Enterprise create real value for those we care about? | **Making a Difference** What can we do to improve and promote the quality of life of those within our community? |
| LEGACY | **Sharing My Values** What of my accomplishments and values will help others find their own future success? | **Family Legacy** What of our accomplishments, values, and traditions will the family carry on? | **Enterprise Legacy** What of the Enterprise's accomplishments and values will be perpetuated in the future? | **Heritage of our Community** How can we use our resources as a means of sharing our values with our communities? |

With this clear and thoughtful declaration of what you stand for as expressed in your family mission statement and a fully articulated vision of what you want going forward, you will be better able to achieve true success as *you* define it.

Let's look at how Carl and Victoria Nelson filled out their grid.

**The Nelsons Begin to Imagine What Could Be**

Once the Nelsons had completed their family mission statement, we met with Carl and Victoria to conduct the vision interview. The interview guide serves as the roadmap for this conversation.

We began the interview by asking what they each liked to do for fun. Victoria had a long litany of the usual suspects: exercising, eating healthy, playing with their grandkids, going out to dinner with Carl, having friends over for dinner, and reading. All well and good.

I then asked her about some of the things she would like to do in the years to come, especially after Carl retired. Victoria had clearly been thinking about this; she immediately started describing the many trips she hoped they would be able to take as a couple, ideally some with their kids, their spouses, and the grandkids. She also talked about wanting to find a leisure activity that she and Carl could do together once he retired.

Finally I asked what she would do to enjoy life in a world where she had infinite resources. If the sky was the limit, what would she want or do? She thought briefly and then said she wished they could have a family vacation home in the Colorado Rockies. She explained this was a dream of her father's. She wanted to fulfill that dream as a way of honoring what he had done for her.

His dream, now her dream, was to have a place big enough for the whole family to be together. This supported one of the important tenets of the family mission: unity. This serves as a good example of how the success mapping process can link vision with family mission.

I began by asking them what it would take to make this dream a reality. Since money wasn't a problem I wanted to know what else they would need to make this happen. Victoria said the house would have to be something the kids would all want to be a part of in the years to come. I pointed out that this could become a very important linchpin in the family's efforts to perpetuate their legacy.

The more we talked about the vacation house, the more excited Carl and Victoria got. They started thinking about the possibilities of tomorrow rather than the constraints of today. I asked them to imagine what it would look like to have everyone together in this mountain hideaway. Victoria talked about the generations sitting in the great room next to the crackling fire, looking out over the beautiful snow-covered peaks, watching the sun set.

Their dream was beginning to take shape as they talked more about the house. I told them we would develop a strategy for this metric of success in an upcoming meeting. Then I asked them to dream some more.

I turned to Carl and asked him to talk about his eventual retirement and the idea of transitioning management of the business to someone outside the family. He expressed his concern that no one, family member or outsider, could be as passionate about the business as he was. When I asked him why, he explained that he was there more than anyone else, usually 65 hours a week. He wasn't sure he could find someone to work as hard as he did.

As we talked about his belief that this grueling schedule was directly responsible for the success and growth of the business, I pointed out that it probably left little time for other activities. Perhaps he could focus on quality time at work rather than quantity time? He agreed, acknowledging that he didn't have a lot of free time and that he was probably asking too much of himself. He ruefully said that maybe this is why none of his kids want to take over the company.

As we listened to Carl, we could sense he was beginning to realize the weight of the time demands he placed on himself was causing him to lose sight of what he wanted of life. This is another powerful characteristic of success mapping: It can help you understand where your life is out of balance.

A change was necessary, Carl realized. He said that although he wanted to see his business continue to grow and be profitable, he now wanted to encourage the next leader to focus only on his or her strengths, delegating everything else to a management team.

I suggested that it might be a good time for Carl to make this change for himself.

He sat there for a minute and then got a big smile on his face. He said that maybe one of the kids might want to succeed him if the workload was closer to what a mere mortal would be expected to do. We all laughed.

Then he said something that surprised Victoria. He said that he wanted to retire at the end of the year. Up until that moment, Carl had refused to say when he imagined retiring. He would always deflect the question saying that he'd know when it's time. Victoria asked him why he now thought he was ready. He replied that he finally knew what he was going to retire *to.*

Carl was excited about the idea of working on plans for the mountain retreat with Victoria. They decided to build a new home rather than search for something they both felt probably didn't exist. This was to be their dream, not someone else's.

I then asked Carl and Victoria to talk about their vision for the business. This is the dimension of success that brought them to Coppertree.

**The Vision for CVN Manufacturing**

I asked Carl and Victoria to think about the future of the business and the perpetuation of the family's legacy. Were they intertwined? They both said yes.

I asked them what happens to the business if the kids don't want to go to work there. Carl replied that the business wouldn't need any of them to run it. I asked him what he thought about the possibility of the kids being owners without necessarily being employees. Carl told us that he hoped the kids would want to continue to own the business regardless of whether they worked for the company or not. I asked him why he wanted them to own the business.

Carl stated his business was very profitable and had much potential in the years to come. He believed the best opportunity to take advantage of this was for the company to stay in the family's hands. He didn't think a strategic buyer would run the company like he did.

He talked about his vision for preserving the culture of the company. He was less interested in quarterly or annual results as he was in letting strategies play out in their own natural time. If something was going to take several years to achieve an objective then so be it.

Furthermore, he understood the business was successful because of the people that worked for him. He knew it was important to keep his highly valued employees and paid them a premium to ensure that.

He believed there was a better chance of the business continuing on as it is if his kids were the owners. They knew what he believed and he hoped they would embrace what he values as the legacy of the business.

Carl noted that it wasn't as if the kids would be selling themselves short by being the next owners of CVN. He said the business was essentially a printing press that printed more money than he could ever generate anywhere else. The kids, as owners, would get a lot of money from this business in the form of distributions.

I summarized what I heard that a metric of success for the Nelson family as owners of CVN was a continuation of the benefits he was receiving from the company. And the legacy of CVN's culture and values had the best chance of carrying on with the Nelsons as owners. I asked Carl and Victoria if that reflected what they wanted for the family and CVN.

Carl said yes.

Victoria said she would love to see the kids be the beneficiaries of Carl's hard work. And she wanted CVN to continue to be a place for its employees to provide for their families and their futures.

There is much more that we cover in the vision interview. Carl and Victoria's vision for success was very extensive. Your vision for success will be too. Figure 4.2 on the next page provides a summary of Carl's vision for success.

This new perspective on what is important and what you want to do will greatly influence how you think about using your resources. It also changes the way you interact with others. Imagine how the conversation changes with your family, your co-workers, or your advisors when you are able to fully describe what matters most and what your vision for success means to you.

**Dreaming Big**

Several years ago a group of wealthy families who were beginning to explore the idea of thinking strategically about using their resources asked us to demonstrate how success mapping could help them.

Todd volunteered to go through a sample success mapping interview. We asked him to describe what he enjoyed doing with his family. Todd was married and had two young daughters, 9 and 11. He rattled off an extensive list, including family vacations, going to the pool, going out to dinner, and many other similar activities.

Then I asked him to dream big—to share a vision of something new he wanted to do that would be fun for his family. After thinking about it a few moments, he said: "I wish I could do what Teddy Roosevelt's parents did when he was a young boy. They took the whole family on a round-the-world trip for a year, to sightsee and learn."

"What's stopping you?" I asked. Money wasn't a concern. He began enumerating his reasons. "The kids need to go to school." Hire a tutor to accompany you, I suggested. "I have to oversee my family businesses." I asked him if he had a management team that could run the businesses while he was away.

Finally, he looked up at me. "Maybe we *could* do this after all." He went on to say that it had always seemed such a far-fetched idea because of all the hurdles he would need to overcome.

"You can do this trip if you put your mind to it," I told him. Later that year someone who was in the meeting that day called to tell me that Todd and his family had decided to do their world trip starting the following summer.

And Todd himself recently called to thank me and to tell me how powerful the experience was for his family. As we said our good-byes, I reminded him that you have to dream big before you can begin to truly pursue what matters most to you.

**What This Means For You**

Taking the time to articulate what you want in life is the next step of living a legacy that lasts. Knowing where you want to go, what you want to do, and what this means to you makes it much easier to decide how you will use your resources to achieve what matters most to you.

What is your vision? Where will your journey take you?

**Figure 4.2 / Carl Nelson's Vision for Success**

| SELF | FAMILY | OUR ENTERPRISE | COMMUNITY |
|---|---|---|---|
| **Enjoying Life** | **Family Enjoyment** | **Supporting the family** | **Community Activities** |
| Organize Weekend Bike Rides | Vacation Home in the Rockies | Establish annual distribution policy | Attend Le Diner en Blanc as Family |
| Get in shape with personal trainer | Summer picnics at the lake | Ownership succession plan for family members | Season ticket/suite for MLB and NFL |
| Cooking school | Family trip to China | Update buy/sell agreement | |
| Be more involved with my church community | | Meet with the board | |
| Anniversary trip June 2016 to Europe | | | |
| **Goals / Accomplishments** | **Family Goals** | **Company Goals** | **Good Citizenry** |
| Retire by year-end | Set up 529 plans for each of the grandkids | Organic growth plan | Volunteer for Judge Smith re- election campaign |
| Buy farm property | Work with legal team on everyone's estate plans regarding the company | Acquisition growth plan | County park board |
| | Set up family blog | Management succession plan | |
| | | Review new product and service ideas | |

| Making a Difference | Family Impact | Stakeholder impact | Making a Difference |
|---|---|---|---|
| Write the book about my journey | Set up family bank for new family ventures | Retirement plan review | Join capital campaign committee for Community Theatre renovation |
| One day excursions with each of the grandkids | Long-range plan for business's ability to support the next 3 generations' interests | Employee training program | Eden Hills Academy Upper School Capital Campaign |
| Spousal Weekend personal growth retreat | | New internship programs | Empower Our Community Program |
| Keynote speech at the Association's Annual Conference | | New social media campaign | |

| Sharing My Values | Family Legacy | Company Legacy | Community Heritage |
|---|---|---|---|
| Sharing family stories | Update the Family Continuity Plan | Create company video | Work with Historical Society on new exhibit celebrating innovation |
| Lunch with all the grandkids to share my dreams for them | Conduct Family Meeting to determine our Family Philanthropy goals | Founder's video — *The Power of Entrepreneurialism in America* | Uptown rejuvenation project |
| Monthly dinners with each of the kids | Review and make Philanthropic Grants | Engage in significant community charity event | |
| Story-telling at annual family meeting | | Property improvement plan | |

/ PART THREE /

# How to Use What You Have to Live a Legacy that Lasts

/ 5 /

# Boundaries Between the Family and the Enterprise

Boundaries exist everywhere in our lives. For example, boundaries represent limits we are asked to honor in a relationship. Boundaries also come in the form of laws designed to protect us or those around us. Boundaries can also be rules that define how we are expected to behave or act within a group.

Much of our work at Coppertree focuses on helping our clients function within and between groups of people. We refer to these groupings as systems. Systems are interactive collections of individuals with a shared bond or purpose. The most common system we encounter is the family. Why do boundaries in families matter?

**Planning for the Future of the Family and the Business**

Where does the responsibility of the business to provide for the family begin and end? The natural tendency of a family is to grow. The business must grow along with the family if it is to meet the family's needs.

There are business-owning families in Europe that have reached the ninth and tenth generations. The business enterprises of Germany's Haniel family, with close to 1,000 living family members, are estimated to generate over $4 billion (USD) in annual profits. The original business in the late 1700s was a merchant trading company.

Over time, the enterprise grew and diversified into many other lines of business. The key to their success: The owners honor the idea that they are family.

This is a symbiotic relationship between two naturally dependent systems. The family owns the business and has capital at risk for which they expect a return on their investment. The business needs the family's capital to invest in profit-making ventures so that it can provide an income stream to the family. It also needs to retain some of the profits to reinvest back into the company for growth. Neither lives without the other. Each must be respectful of the other.

As long as a mutual respect for each other's needs exists between the family and the business, the prospects for a prosperous future are bright. Where families and the managers of the business get in trouble is when one system disagrees with or ignores the needs of the other.

The boundaries at play in the Preston Family are a case in point.

**Family Wants versus Business Needs**

Paula Preston's family owned and operated more than 40 franchise stores of a leading fast food chain that was passed down from her father's estate. Paula's father Ralph Marak was one of the original franchisees of the chain.

Thanks to the shrewd advice of the family's estate-planning attorney, Ralph had transferred his ownership of the restaurants into a multi-generational trust. The trust would benefit the family for a very long time without an untoward burden of estate taxes as each generation passed on. Paula's parents died in the late 1990s. As their only child, Paula was the sole beneficiary of her parents' estate.

Paula and her husband Joe had two sons and two daughters in their 30s. The Preston's oldest children were not employed in the business. Their youngest child, Erin, after completing a highly regarded graduate program in economics, fulfilled a life-long dream and joined the business. All of the children, however, were now beneficial owners of the generational trust along with their mother, Paula.

Erin always wanted to be involved with the management of the family's restaurant business. During high school and college she would work in the stores on evenings and weekends. After completing her graduate studies she started working on the corporate strategy team in the franchise group's business office. She hoped she would be able to succeed her mother as CEO someday.

Erin's father also worked in the business, as CFO. His primary focus was expanding their franchise locations through land acquisition. But this organic growth strategy was showing less and less promise as real estate prices in Southern California continued to soar.

Erin saw a different avenue to growth. Having met several of the other franchise group owners in her region, she could see that many of these individuals were now in their late 70s and looking to get out of the restaurant business. She saw an opportunity to buy out some of these elderly owners. This was frowned on by the chain's corporate leadership, however, because they didn't want too much power in the hands of any single franchise group.

Erin convinced her parents the best opportunity to grow their business as a multi-generational legacy asset was to pursue her strategy of buying out other franchise owners. Erin and her parents met with management at the corporate offices and eventually convinced them that it was in the best interest of the company to allow the Prestons to pursue their strategy as long as their strategy was well-financed and supported by their banks.

**Planning for the Future of the Business**

Sometimes it is far easier to judge and be critical of others' ideas than it is to accept and stay neutral. This is especially true within a family. We each see the world and each other through our own set of filters, filters created by a lifetime of experiences as a member of our family. Many of these experiences shape how the family sees the world and each other. When our personal views are out of sync with family views conflict often results.

Family members want others in the family to respect their view or opinion. We set boundaries to keep us safe from harmful conflict by limiting what we will tolerate when dealing with opposing views. In respecting each other's boundaries as issues are considered, compromises can be reached and decisions made.

Thanks to their franchise's success Paula and Joe's children grew up in an affluent neighborhood and lived a luxurious life. However, money was a taboo subject that was not to be discussed. Paula and Joe chose not to tell their children where all of the money came from to fund their lifestyle. When they were young the kids knew their parents owned many locations of this world-famous chain. They had no clue the restaurants were the source of the family's wealth. All they knew was that money never seemed to be an issue for their family.

Paula and Joe's children could have benefited from participating in a family business education program. There they would have learned about how family and business interact and what the needs are of each other. In this way they could have better understood that the business was not an endless source of cash to be given to the family. The limit or boundary on expectations could have been established through this process.

To move forward with her plan, Erin would have to convince her siblings that her strategy was in their best interest as well. Because of the ownership structure that Paula's father had established, Erin and her siblings collectively controlled the business as beneficial owners of the family trust. They were also income beneficiaries of the trust at this point. Each beneficiary received 20 percent of any distributions from the trust.

The trust income was very important to two of Erin's siblings who had become "trust fund babies." Their lavish lifestyles were largely supported by the quarterly distributions from the trust. Any reduction in distributions would not be taken lightly by these two sibs.

Herein lay the problem. Erin's siblings' need for current income from the trust conflicted with the legacy goal of creating and sustaining wealth for present and future generations of the family.

But if Erin were to have any chance of financing her purchase of the other franchise groups, she would need to severely curtail the current distributions to her siblings and herself. She would also need to borrow substantial sums from banks and other lending institutions.

Would they be willing to give up some or all of their current trust income and would they be comfortable with the substantial risk Erin's venture would expose the family to? She expected the long-term benefits of her strategy would be far greater than the temporary, short-term reduction in trust income. Would the family be willing to move ahead with Erin's plan?

For the good of the family the business would need to grow. For the business to grow, the enterprise's owners would have to be willing to take less cash out of the business. This is an important and typical crossroad that many business owning families face at some point along the journey.

For the Prestons this would be no easy decision. Would it be possible to satisfy the needs of the family members and the business at the same time? It is my belief that both the family's needs and the enterprise's needs could be addressed simultaneously as long as they were within reason.

In the case of the Prestons it would not be possible to maintain trust distributions at the level they had been accustomed to if the acquisition strategy was pursued. This presents another system boundary issue to consider for families such as the Prestons. Each system or group has its own needs and expectations of the other as illustrated in Figure 5.1.

Would it be wise for Erin to simply spring the news on the family that she planned to redirect the cash flow used for trust distributions to funding her acquisition strategy? Would it be worthwhile to present this idea to the family well in advance of initiating it, especially because of the burden it would place on her siblings?

Transparency and communication are the keys to keeping this family together. The more Erin and her management team can do to help the family understand what she wants to do, the greater the likelihood will be in getting her family's buy-in. This is also an illustration of the need for the family to have a family mission and vision as the basis for making decisions as a family.

## The Contributing Factors

The Preston family's situation can be seen as an accident waiting to happen. A chain of events over time created the conflict Erin was confronted with between the boundaries of her family and the family business.

Erin and her siblings weren't told the family story when they were young. They didn't know what their grandfather went through to

**Figure 5.1**

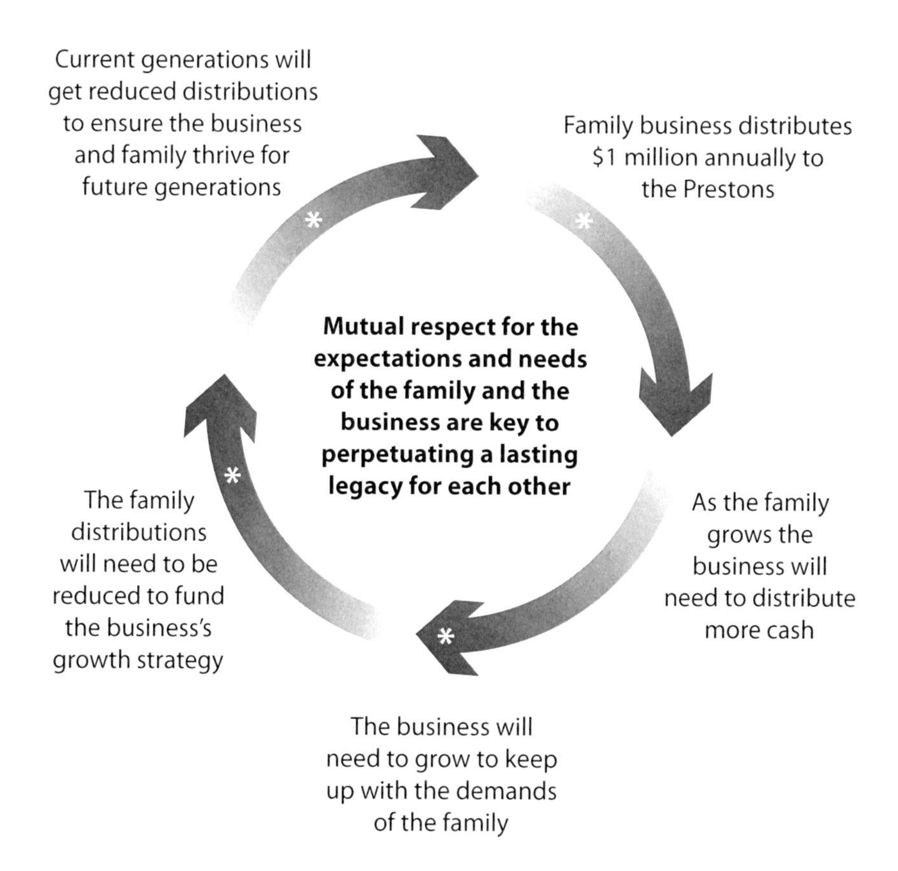


achieve his successes or why he owned these businesses and how this ownership shaped his dreams for his family. It would've been better for Paula and Joe to share the family story with Erin and her siblings so they would have an understanding of what the family valued as a basis for making decisions with respect to their enterprise.

Paula and Joe chose not to talk about the money they made nor what the family would inherit from Paula's father. Paula and Joe believed it would be better to keep their children in the dark about how wealthy the family was rather than risk what most wealthy families worry about: that the money would destroy their children's lives. It would've been better to provide financial education to Paula and Joe's children to avert the eventual dependence of Erin's siblings on the trust distributions. They had little understanding of the "money" side of wealth. Where did it come from? What were the responsibilities of wealth? How were you supposed to use it and interact with it? They were financially illiterate.

This chain of events and beliefs put the Preston family in a precarious situation. Ignorance, selfishness, a lack of purpose and understanding of what needed to be done all contributed.

Certainly the business existed to benefit the family. But the family needed to perpetuate the family legacy by growing the business for future generations of the family. Some of the profits could be reinvested into the franchise operation or could be invested in new ventures if they were deemed more appropriate.

A combination of poor communication, no established forum for dealing with family affairs, a lack of clarity on the family's values, and no mechanism to prepare and position family members for the future all contributed.

Erin was unable to convince her siblings that the enterprise's capacity to perpetuate the family's wealth was in jeopardy. The franchise was eventually sold to a good friend of Erin's whose family was doing exactly what Erin had hoped to do with her family's franchise: grow through acquisition. Although Erin and her siblings would be able to live out their lives in the privileged manner they were born to, the family's legacy wealth didn't grow enough to afford their children the same life of luxury.

A respect for the boundaries of interaction between the family and the business will greatly influence the success or failure of such a family. Violations of boundaries are where conflicts occur. Some

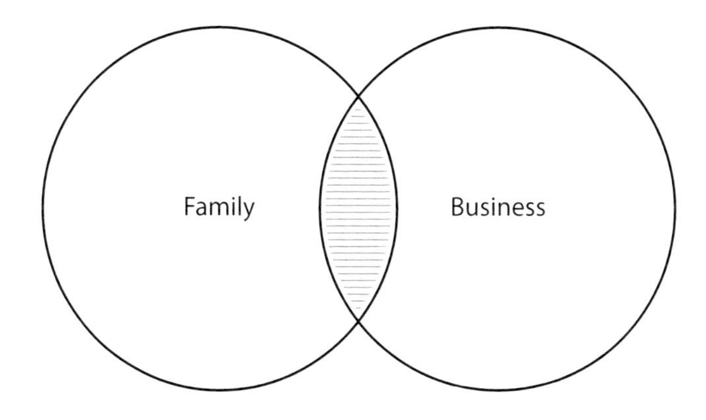

families don't think of these issues as boundary issues. They are boundary issues in the sense that the two systems have an overlapping zone where they interact with each other. When systems interact, this can cause conflict unless a family is prepared to deal with such issues. The impact of a decision in one system can influence any system that interacts with it.

---

**Coppertree's Perspective:**
**The Dynamic of Family—The Fourth Dimension**

A widely cited model has been used by business-owning families and their advisors to better understand and manage the transactions related to change issues. The model depicts the dimensions within a family business in the form of a three-circle Venn diagram that represents the business, its owners, and the family itself. The overlaps between the circles represent the areas where change in one dimension can produce change in the other dimensions as well.[3]

A new interpretation of this model with the addition of a fourth dimension gives families a new framework to manage the process of change that will enable them to perpetuate their legacy across generations.

The family business system model can be expanded to consider the dynamics of any family enterprise, be it a business, family foundation, or vacation property. The new vocabulary for the Family Enterprise Four-Dimension Framework is:

- Business is more broadly viewed as Money—the family enterprise legacy asset in whatever form it exists
- Ownership as a component of Power—ownership and control of the enterprise can be separate considerations.
- Family issues are a function of Relationships—the interconnectedness of individuals whether they are family members or not.

The fourth dimension, the Family Dynamic, emerges from the family's multi-generational journey and each family member's own unique story.

This is the force that manages or mismanages change in the enterprise and in the family unit.

If the stakeholders within the money and power dimensions do not take into consideration the family story, values, and individual goals, those entities will more than likely not succeed. However, if time is

---

3 R. Taguri and J. A. Davis, "Bivalent Attributes of the Family Firm," *Family Business Review*, vol. 9, no. 2, 1996, pp. 199–208.

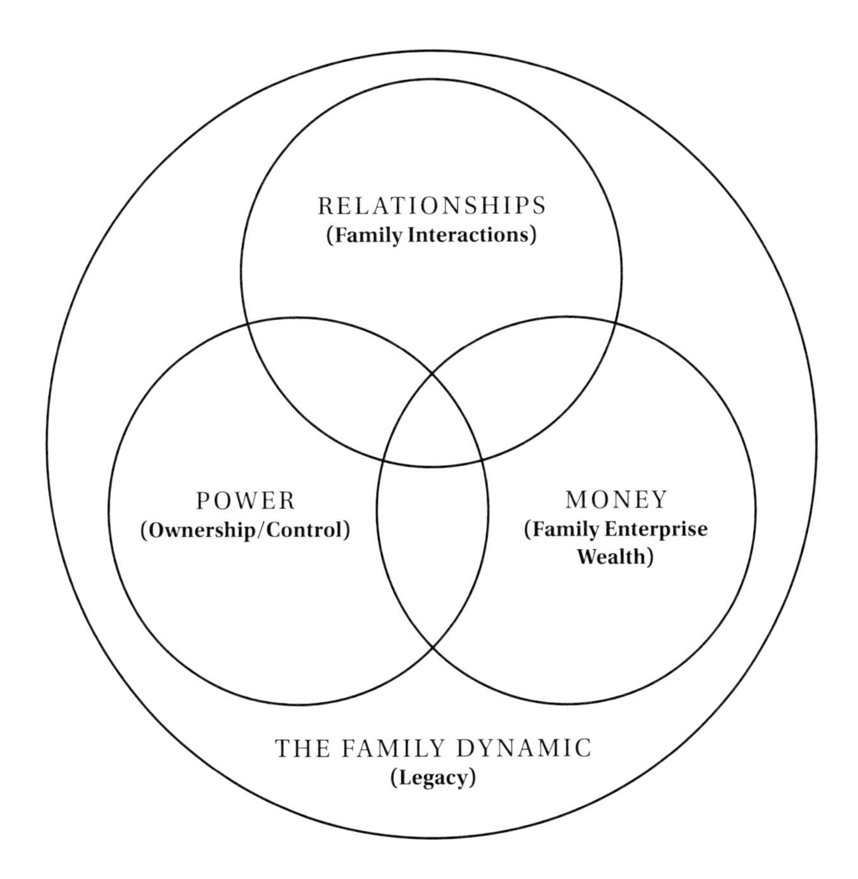


taken, using the success mapping process, to decide how the family will proactively meet expected developmental changes or handle unexpected changes, they will be better equipped to call on their articulated shared values to accept change as it occurs.

Change is natural. Families can be better prepared for managing the process of change by knowing how the family dynamic can be used as a positive force to meet challenges head on, empowering the family to make good, shared, purpose-driven decisions.

## What This Means For You

Enterprise owning families and their business are two separate but interacting systems. Each serves the other and receives benefits in return. The areas of interaction between the overlapping boundaries of the family system and the business system are fruitful grounds for living a legacy defined by success or failure.

Families who have an appreciation for the need to manage this interaction in a mutually respectful manner between the family's expectations and the enterprise's prerequisite to grow have a greater likelihood that both will thrive well into the future.

Does your family have realistic expectations of what they want and need from the enterprise? Does your enterprise financially reward the family for the risks they take in owning the business?

/ 6 /

# Governance

## MAKING FAMILY DECISIONS

In your work life, do you make decisions alone and on a whim? If you own a business, do you have a process for making decisions? Most likely, the decisions you make are well thought out, the result of a refined process based on a plan developed to guide you along the way.

What about the decisions you make as a family? Many families are like the pilots of old when it comes to making family decisions. They fly by the seat of their pants.

In the early days of aviation, a pilot actually flew his plane in response to how the aircraft's movements were shifting him around in his seat. The first airplanes had few instruments. Nor did pilots have navigational maps or operating manuals to augment their skills. You simply flew based on what felt right, improvising as you went along—flying by the seat of your pants.

Today, airplane manufacturers provide pilots with a Pilot's Operating Handbook (POH) for their plane which consists of many interacting, complex systems. The POH is essentially a step-by-step guide for operating the plane. From pre-flight inspections to start-up routines to normal flight operations to emergency procedures, the POH gives the pilot all the information needed to handle the various aspects of flying the plane safely and successfully.

As in aviation, families making decisions are at great risk of a bad outcome if they fly by the seat of their pants. A guide for family decision-making based on processes to manage the interacting systems of enterprise owning families is broadly referred to as a *family governance system.*

What happens when families don't have a good governance plan in place to manage the interaction of the family system, the business system, and the ownership system that are typically at play?

In 2014 third and fourth generation family members who co-owned a well known business in Ohio went to war. One branch of the family accused another of taking advantage of their positions as employees of the business by overpaying themselves and wasting corporate resources. They ultimately filed lawsuits to rectify the problem.

Media accounts suggested that a lack of transparency and poor communication led to the conflict. It was unlikely the family had anything in place to guide them on how they should function as co-owners, employees, and beneficiaries of their enterprise. What might this guide look like and how could it have been used to avert the conflict?

Of all the aspects of success mapping, family governance is the most straightforward, yet oftentimes the most contentious. Everyone in the family has an opinion on how best to run the family's affairs. A governance system provides an administrative framework. Clarity is key. For example what do we really mean when we talk about family membership? Who, what, where, when, why, and how do we come together to discuss the affairs of the family?

A family governance system is for families what government is for countries. So let's look at James Madison's explanation of the U.S. government as a self-governing system: "If men were angels, no government would be necessary. [. . .] In framing a government which is to be administered by men over men, the great difficulty lies in this: you must first enable the government to control the governed; and in the next place oblige it to control itself." (Federalist Paper No. 51, 1788)

How would we apply Madison's explanation to families? It might go something like this: "If families were perfect, no family governance system would be necessary. In framing a family governance system which is to be administered by family members for family members, the great difficulty lies in this: you must first enable the family leaders to control the family; and in the next place oblige them to control themselves."

As our country's founders recognized, laws (rules) make living in groups manageable. Families who adopt a set of rules to serve as a guide in making decisions together find they minimize conflict and stress.

---

**Jenny's View: The Governance Continuum**

What happens when someone in the family, who is a co-owner of a family business, wants to share their opinion with the management of the company on improving the business's performance? Imagine this individual is a member of the 4th Generation of this family: one of seventy. Is it fair to the business's managers to be expected to respond to every suggestion and idea that any of these 70 owners may present as a mandate? Is it any less fair for family members to be precluded from having a voice in formulating the family's expectations of the business they own?

The interaction between a family and their business is best managed by incorporating two intermediaries placed between the family and their business: a family council and a board of advisors/directors.

The family council serves as the representative body on behalf of the family. A board of advisors or board of directors are charged with

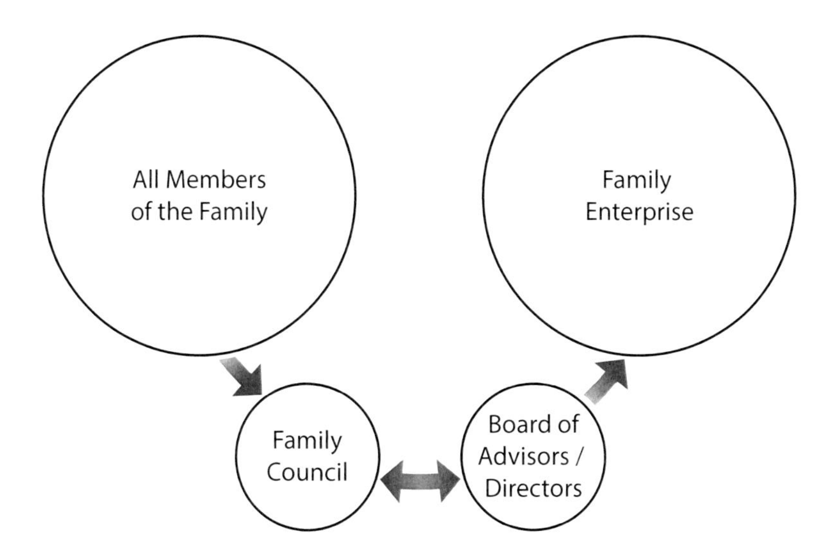

overseeing the enterprise's managers and their performance on behalf of the owners of the business.

Family members select their representatives as determined by the family governance plan who in turn appoint individuals to serve on the board. In this manner, both family and enterprise have a mechanism for communicating with each other efficiently. No one is left out of the conversation. Everyone is heard.

Business-owning families will usually have some pieces of a governance plan in place in the form of an operating agreement or bylaws for their company. Or an estate plan may exist. But these plans don't necessarily give guidance to the family in making decisions based on their vision for the future. Nor is a family governance system a substitute for an operating agreement or estate plan. A family governance system serves as the basis for estate plans and operating agreements.

A family governance system would address issues such as the definition of a family member. For some families this is limited to direct descendants of the founding member of the family. For others it might include spouses. What happens when someone is divorced? Do they lose their status as a family member if they are not a descendent? How are adopted children treated?

### Outline of Family Governance Plans

Family governance plans (also known as constitutions, charters, or bylaws) generally cover issues relating to a co-owned enterprise such as a business, foundation, or resort property. It would include sections such as:

***Purpose and structure***

- This section explains how the family's values and goals are to guide decision-making. It details the structure of the family's decision-making body, typically a family council. This section would list the long-term multigenerational objectives of the family. The section would conclude with the family's position on retention or disposition of family enterprises in the future.

***Family membership and enterprise ownership***

- This section addresses the family's criteria for being recognized as a family member and eligibility requirements to be an owner of controlling or noncontrolling interests in family enterprises. This section also describes the process for ownership transition (augmented by the legal remedies set forth in the appropriate governing documents of the enterprise). Divorce and adoption would be covered in this section.

***Employment, compensation, career advancement***

- This section states the requirements for family member employment in family enterprises, including academic credentials, prior work experience, and demonstrated ability to manage others. It sets forth the criteria for compensation and advancement in the company. This section also addresses the requirements to be considered for promotion as well as remediation measures for underperforming family members.

***Family leadership***

- Just as in the enterprise, a well-functioning family will have a plan and criteria in place to select each successive generation's leaders. This section would also outline the rules, roles, and responsibilities of family members who serve on the family council.

Let's turn our attention to the Nelson family once again to see how the governance planning process works:

### A Framework for Managing Expectations

As we continued to meet with Carl and Victoria Nelson, I explained the importance of establishing rules and procedures to guide the family in making decisions and I asked them to describe what they had in place.

Carl had been transferring equal interests of his ownership into trusts for each of their five children and their descendants. In this way, each branch would have an equal say as owners. We refer to this as a *legacy ownership structure*. His law firm's tax specialist had set up the transfer strategy, which would also reduce the family's eventual estate tax liability.

I told Carl this sounded like a well-thought-out plan that reflected what he was trying to do for his family, then asked him what he had communicated with the kids about the management and ownership of the business.

Carl told each of them they would have an opportunity to succeed him if they had the desire and the qualifications. He also made it clear to them that ownership was different from management. As owners, they would have the power to appoint people to their board whose responsibility was to provide guidance to the CEO with respect to the owners' expectations, but their power stopped there. In his mind unless they were employed in the business, they weren't allowed to meddle in management.

I then asked Carl what would happen if one of the kids wants out.

Carl asked what I meant by *wanting out.*

What would he do if one of the kids decided to sell their interest in the business? What could they do?

Carl became quite agitated and said they'd take a bath. He explained the operating agreement was set up to discourage anyone from selling their interest. They could sell, but only at a very deep discount to what their share of the business is actually worth.

I asked him what he thought this would do to his dream of the family staying together.

Carl thought for a moment, then said that it would cause some very hard feelings. It would probably be the beginning of the end of the family.

I asked him if this is what he wanted.

He said no, but he didn't know what he could do to preserve the business and perpetuate the family legacy at the same time.

This is where a well-written family governance plan can help.

He wanted to know why he would need such a plan if he already had an operating agreement for the business, a gifting plan for the company stock, and an estate plan.

I asked him which of these documents would guide his kids in how they could interact with the business, either as owners, beneficiaries, or employees. Which of these documents would provide guidance to the kids on family meetings to discuss the business and the family? To discuss, for example, a family member's decision to put their interest up for sale? I explained that the governance plan was an operating manual and bylaws all rolled into one.

Carl conceded and asked what needed to be done to create a governance plan for his family.

I explained that he's halfway home having already worked on the values and vision components of the success mapping process. Knowing the values you want to uphold and perpetuate along with understanding where you want to go gives us the foundation of the governance plan. We established the structure, systems, and processes the Nelsons would use to make purpose-driven decisions on behalf of the family and created their governance plan (Figure 6.1) which they referred to as a charter.

---

***Figure 6.1***
**The Carl & Victoria Nelson Family Charter**

**Purpose**

The Nelson Family Charter has been created in response to our family's need to make joint decisions and to set forth the responsibilities, obligations, and privileges associated with membership in our family. Our family charter is intended to provide tactical guidance in the execution of our Family Continuity Plan.

**Family Membership**

Membership in the Nelson family extends to all natural descendants of Carl and Victoria Nelson, their spouses, domestic partners, children adopted before the age of 21, and stepchildren entering the family before the age of 21.

Each of Carl and Victoria Nelson's natural children and their family members as described above have been designated as separate Nelson Family Branches. The Family Assembly comprises all family members (as described above). Voting members of the family include all family members (as described above) who have reached the age of 25.

**Responsibilities**

Family members are expected to stay fully informed of the family enterprise activities by reviewing all updates, reports, reviews, and recommendations presented by the Family Council. Furthermore, family members are required to participate in the Family Assembly each June.

**Communication**

The Nelson family understands the importance of communication within the family. Regular communication throughout the family is conducted via formal channels such as the family blog, quarterly enterprise updates, and the Annual Review. Informal contact within the family is also crucial to keeping the family informed and connected. Family members are strongly encouraged to actively share their experiences with the family as they journey through life, giving the family an opportunity to recognize and celebrate each member's individual accomplishments.

**Code of Conduct**

Family members are expected to treat all members of the family with love, respect, compassion, and tolerance toward individual views and philosophies. Family members are expected to support and encourage every member of the family in their pursuit of health, happiness, and success. The family's multigenerational goal is to promote and nurture unity within the family.

Family members are expected to collaborate fairly and honestly, to treat each other with respect, and to honor family confidentiality. Family members should strive for mutual understanding in family discussions. Family members are encouraged to weigh the potential consequences of each family negotiation before we decide how much energy and time the situation merits.

Family members are expected to be mutually supportive, to know ourselves and each other as best we can, to sort out misunderstandings where we see them, and to request further information when a family member's position is unclear. Family members are urged to consider family disputes with care, to do our best to keep them from causing serious family rifts, and to empower family elders to act as arbiters in their ultimate resolution.

Family members are expected to act with dignity and integrity in dealing with the outside world.

**Family Assembly**

The purpose of the Family Assembly is to review and assess existing family enterprise activities in the context of macroeconomic conditions and new enterprise opportunities such as:

- Ensuring that distributions to family are based on business performance and capital needs of the business
- Collaborating with the CVN Manufacturing's Board of Directors to advise on all transitions of family leadership and family enterprise leadership
- Reviewing and assessing the activities of the Nelson Family Foundation

The Nelson Family Assembly is held beginning at noon on the first Thursday of June and concludes at noon on the following day. The Nelson Family Annual Meeting begins immediately following the conclusion of the Family Assembly and concludes with the Nelson Family Annual Banquet beginning at 6 o'clock the following evening.

Every member of the family must attend the Family Assembly. Only voting members of the family may participate (vote) in the decision-making aspects of the Assembly. All family members and non-members who are approved by the Family Council may attend the Nelson Family Annual Meeting.

**Annual Family Meeting**

The purpose of the Nelson Family Annual Meeting is to bring the entire family together to celebrate individual and collective family accomplishments from the past year, such as:

- Gaining additional insight through storytelling into the family's values that were shaped by the family's history and heritage
- Providing age-specific educational programs for personal growth and understanding with regard to the family's enterprises
- Affirming and seating new members of the Family Council for the coming term

The Annual Family Meeting is also considered to be a family reunion—a time to get to know each other, renew old bonds, and forge new ones.

Family members should attend the Nelson Family Annual Meeting and Family Assembly in person. However, in special circumstances family members are permitted to participate via a video-conference link if they are unable to attend in person. Family members are permitted one excused absence every five years. Failure to actively participate in four out of five rolling meetings will result in loss of voting privileges pertaining to family enterprise affairs for the three years following violation of the attendance policy.

**Family Council**

The purpose of the Family Council is to represent and protect the family's interests in the family enterprises beyond the Family Assembly. The Family Council is expected to disseminate information pertaining to the family enterprises such as financial and management reports to all family members monthly and quarterly. The Family Council is also responsible for overseeing the execution of succession plans for leadership of the family enterprises as representative shareholders.

The Family Council consists of up to three voting members for each family branch. Carl and Victoria Nelson are lifetime voting members of the Family Council. Voting family members within each branch elect their branch's Family Council members. Each of Carl and Victoria's children is the head of a branch of the family in this regard.

Family Council members are to be elected to serve for two years and may be re-elected once before rotating off the Council for at least one term. Family Council elections should be staggered every three years.

A Family Council member may be removed prior to the end of his or her term by a majority vote of Council members and a plurality of family members. Such removal should follow only from manifest malfeasance or negligence on the part of the member in question.

The chair for the Family Council is to be selected by Council members at the Family Assembly each year. The chair's responsibilities include preparing the agendas and presiding over meetings.

Family Council meetings are held from 9:00 AM to 5:00 PM on the first Friday of March, September, and December. The purpose of the Council meetings is to review the affairs of the family enterprises and to address any other business that may come before the Family Council.

Attendance at Family Council meetings by Council members is mandatory. Any voting member of the family is also welcome to attend Council meetings. Council members serve as proxies for their family branch and as such are authorized to make decisions on behalf of the family at large during the family enterprise meetings. Other voting members present are invited to participate in discussions but are not permitted to cast a vote on resolutions brought forth at Family Council meetings.

Family Council members are expected to participate in every Council meeting in person. However, in special circumstances Council members are permitted to participate via a video-conference link if they are unable to attend the meeting in person. Council members are permitted one absence during each two-year term. Failure to actively participate in more than one meeting will result in loss of voting privileges pertaining to family enterprise affairs for the remainder of the Council member's term. All Council members must keep in mind that they represent the voice of their family branch and therefore have the responsibility to act on behalf of their branch.

Travel and related expenses incurred by Family Council members and invited guests attending Council meetings will be fully reimbursed from an enterprise resource.

**Family Elders**

The Nelson family believes that our family elders possess a wisdom that can greatly add to the sustainability of the family, especially in times of conflict or uncertainty. The family has agreed to defer to the prudence of the family elders when consensus is not reached with regard to important issues.

The family elders consist of three family members who are selected for life by the voting members of the Family Assembly. Family elders can be removed from their role by a supermajority (three-fourths of all voting members) of the Family Assembly.

The family elders can be called on to serve as mediators in addressing unresolved family issues. The decision of the Family Elders is final and irrefutable.

**Family Member Personal Development and Opportunities**

All family members are expected to pursue and complete the highest level of education that is appropriate for their circumstances. Each family branch is encouraged to use the resources of the educational trust created for each branch to fund educational pursuits by that branch's family members.

Family members, having achieved their highest level of appropriate education, will be given opportunities to pursue positions within family enterprises that are appropriate to their capabilities. Family members choosing to limit their educational achievements will not be invited to participate in the family enterprises.

**Family Enterprise Employment**

Family members are encouraged to take active roles and positions in the family enterprises.

In order to be considered for any family enterprise leadership positions, family members are expected to:

- Earn a college degree
- Be employed by a non-family enterprise for at least five years
- Enter the family enterprise at a level commensurate with experience and according to qualification for the position
- Be hired only where and when a genuine job is available
- Receive initial compensation based on company standards with increases based on merit
- Agree to termination decisions made by direct superiors based on performance

- Agree to the general terms of employment for the enterprise's non-family employees

Family members without college degrees will be given the opportunity to pursue non-leadership positions at a level commensurate with experience and according to qualification for the position.

Family members seeking career opportunities in the family enterprise will also be given opportunities to participate in internships. Non-family senior-level managers will be available to serve as mentors to family members throughout their career development process.

**Ownership Interests**

Family member ownership is voluntary. All family members wishing to divest themselves of their interests in the family enterprise may liquidate their interest via the terms of the ownership agreements associated with the enterprise.

**Nelson Family Foundation**

The purpose of the Foundation is to give back to our community. Family members' pursuits of their many diverse interests with respect to philanthropic activities are encouraged to the extent that each endeavor reflects the family's wish to support education as empowerment. The Nelson Family Foundation is also viewed as an educational tool for younger members of the family.

The Family Assembly and Family Council are to oversee the mission-based philanthropic initiatives of the Foundation, to recruit tactical input, distribute Foundation updates to the family, and to organize joint philanthropy as both philanthropic leverage for adult members and an educational tool for young members.

**Review, Assessment, and Modification of the Nelson Family Charter**

The Family Charter is a vital component of our family's desire to flourish as a family for many generations. Therefore, the Family Assembly is expected to review and affirm the precepts of the Family Charter annually to ensure its relevance. When necessary, changes and revisions may be incorporated into the Family Charter with approval of three-quarters of voting family members.

**Financial Resource Allocation and Budget**

Each family branch is responsible for managing their personal financial affairs in accordance with the family's goal of growing the family's wealth for generations to come.

**What This Means For You**

How will your family make decisions together regarding co-owned or shared assets? Do you have governance rules and guidelines for your family to use in the decision-making process on family related matters?

Families who take the time to establish a governance plan will find it much easier to make decisions together that will promote harmony while perpetuating the family legacy for generations to come.

/ 7 /

# Structuring the Vision

## PRIORITIES AND RESOURCES

What are you focused on right now? What might the future hold for you? Are you able to think multidimensionally about everything that matters to you?

During my tenure as a financial advisor, I faced two challenges in responding to what mattered most to my clients. The first came from not asking the right questions. The fundamental questions not being asked were, "What matters to you? What does a life well lived look like to you? What do you need to do to pursue what matters most?"

The second challenge is much like assembling a jigsaw puzzle, the whole picture doesn't come into view until every piece of the issue has been placed into its proper position in the puzzle. Additionally, as in a puzzle, each piece of the puzzle is needed for it to be a complete picture. If any piece of the puzzle is missing you end up with less than the full perspective. Similarly for families pursuing what matters, how could all of the various expertise, experience, and resources a family needs to live their legacy be brought together in a singular framework?

In this phase of the success mapping process, we prioritize the myriad measures of success that were identified in the vision phase. We also assess what forms of your life capital will be needed to achieve each metric of success. In the next chapter we will describe how to allocate your life capital and subsequently develop a strategy to use these resources with the help of your advisors in pursuit of what matters most to you and your family.

**Prioritizing Your Measures of Success**

Today, you might be thinking about enjoying time together as family in the routines of ordinary life or perhaps the extraordinary trip of a lifetime. Tomorrow, your focus might shift to finding a new cause to support, allowing you to give back to your world in a way that reflects your personal and family values.

As your interests shift, so does the need to think about what you must do to reach your dreams and goals. Success mapping was designed to help you help yourself, using all the resources available to you in a coordinated and logical way. What might this look like?

How do taking an afternoon bike ride, working on a research project at work, having a conversation with your daughter about a career change, and preparing for an interview with the business editor of a national magazine about the founding of your family business all fit together? On top of that, how do planning a family reunion next summer, growing a business by 25 percent over the next three years, chairing a dinner reception for cancer research next month, and preparing to give a keynote address at an industry conference on the importance of company culture get accomplished at the same time?

As you try to envision how these eight items fit together, they may seem unrelated, random, or even trivial. This list probably doesn't mean anything to you. But it's very real to the person it belongs to because it's everything that matters to that person right now. To anyone else, your list may seem just as random.

Assume for sake of discussion this list is your list. If you think about each of the eight activities listed above, none alone seems unattainable. But, if you had to deal with all of them at the same time, where would you start? Just to make this even more real, what if you were married and your spouse had an equal number of projects of her own?

Want more? Then pile on the additional issues you want to address with your grown children and their families. What if everything needed to be done right now?

Not anxious enough yet? Just to pile a little more fuel on the fire, what if your list was over a hundred items long rather than just eight? Where would you start? What item is more important than any other item?

Everything that matters to most of us is more than we have the capacity to address all at once. Our most valuable personal commodity is time. How should you allocate your time and all other forms of your life capital? Success mapping lays out a strategy that determines what needs to be done, by what date, by whom, along with the resources needed to achieve what matters most to you right now.

The framework of the success mapping process brings everything together and ensures they are properly assembled to pursue what is important in living your legacy.

**Where Do We Start?**

When they look at their success map, most people are overwhelmed by the number of elements they have listed as being important to them. And, of course, they are all important. But you can only do one at a time. As you examine your list, what of your life capital resources should be allocated to each metric of success?

Where do you start? Which measures of success commands your time and attention now and which will have to wait? Based on what is important to you and your family, what is the best way to achieve success in pursuit of all of these interests?

In the visioning interview phase of the success mapping process, individual and family success maps were created (See Figure 4.1). If you're like most individuals who go through the success mapping process, your vision of a well-lived life would include many measures of success. It is not uncommon for an individual to list 50, 60, even 100 or more measures that represent a well-lived life.

As you look at your list, which metric is most important to you right now? Do you want to work on your relationship with your spouse? Or maybe you want to spend more time with your children. You might have something you've been wanting to accomplish in your work life such as starting a business or applying your talents in a different professional pursuit. The key is to identify what is most important to you.

The first step in this phase of the process is to rank each metric of success. The ranking can be based on the timeliness of an issue, its importance, or a combination of both. For example, you may have identified the need to find a successor to lead the business when you retire. In addition, you may have been directed by your doctor to report to the hospital to treat a serious health issue. They are both important. Which one has a more immediate claim on your time today? Looking at the list of eight activities mentioned earlier, which would you consider to be the highest ranked? What if they're similar in nature such as preparing for the interview or writing the keynote address. Which comes first?

What happens when families or family members don't make good choices as they get their priorities out of order as a result of dealing with a single issue while many other issues are not being attended to?

Bruce is a case in point.

### One-Dimensional Bruce

I met Bruce through a mutual friend shortly after I opened the doors to Coppertree. After earning a graduate degree from an Ivy League school, he became a bond trader for a global investment bank, then founded a successful hedge fund in Charlotte.

Two years later it had grown to several billion in assets under management. He was totally consumed with expanding his business.

Bruce was married with two teenage daughters, and was struggling with family issues. His wife had recently informed him that she was considering a divorce because of his workaholic behavior. Bruce was beside himself and was willing to try anything to save his marriage and his family. Our mutual friend thought I could help Bruce think a little differently about what was going on in his life.

During our first meeting I asked Bruce to tell me about what life was like when he was a child. He responded that it didn't really have anything to do with who he was today. I asked him to give me the highlights of his story just the same.

Bruce had grown up in Appalachia, the eldest son of a coal miner. He observed how hard his father worked and the toll it took on him. He was never close to his father who was either at work or drunk.

Bruce told me he promised himself that he'd never be like that, like his father. He'd be a better father and family man. He added that he also vowed he'd never be poor. He told me the day he left the holler, he ran as fast as he could and never looked back.

During our next meeting, I asked him why he thought his wife was considering divorce. He said he really didn't know. He said it wasn't like they were fighting all the time—he usually didn't get home until long after she'd gone to bed.

I repeated back to Bruce what he had just said. He agreed that he was working very long hours. He said that he was wrapping up phone calls with clients and prospects from the West Coast until nine or ten almost every evening, which meant that he wasn't able to get home before eleven most nights.

I asked him how his wife felt about his late nights at the office. He said she was worried about their daughters because they were becoming increasingly distant, and she wished he was home more often to be available to talk to them at such a delicate time in their lives. He tried to explain how important it was for him to be as financially successful as he could, that he hadn't reached his 'number' yet.

I asked him if he thought he had run far enough yet. He asked me what I meant. I reminded him of the comment he'd made the first time we met about running as fast as he could to get away from the poverty of his past.

I commented that it must be tough having to be at the office all the time and not seeing his daughters and being a part of their lives. He started to say something about the nice home he had provided for them when he stopped and looked at me. He realized he'd become his father.

He asked me whether it was too late to make a change.

I asked him how important his family was to him. He said there was nothing more important. They were what mattered. I asked him what he would be willing to change in his life. He said he'd do whatever it would take to win back his family.

Bruce thought for another minute and asked if this meant his business would have to suffer. I asked him whether he was the only person employed at his firm and he said no. I told him I really didn't know what effect his time away from work would have on his business, but this was a good example of the challenge we all face as we prioritize what matters to us.

The moral of the story for Bruce is a simple one: You can't be in two places at once. So where you choose to be now comes at the cost of not being somewhere else.

As his mind opened up and Bruce imagined the possibilities, he started to realize he had a thirst for experiencing all the goodness in his life as it is and as it could be. He began to see that what matters was much more than just his work life.

What really mattered to Bruce was his family. Yet he devoted his resources to a never-ending quest for more money. The framework of the success mapping process gave Bruce an opportunity to think about what mattered to him based on where he came from, where he wanted to go, and what it would take to achieve his dreams using the resources he had available.

Life is complicated and it's easy to get sidetracked much like Bruce did. The success mapping process lets you take complicated, multifaceted, seemingly unrelated issues and synthesizes them into a plan for using your resources in a prioritized manner that makes sense to you—the key to pursuing what matters most to you.

The next step in the process is to determine which and how much of your life capital resources you will need to achieve each of your measures of success.

**Life Capital Defined**

We are all limited by the resources we have available to accomplish what we want to achieve. When I use the word *resources* I'm referring more broadly to *capital.* Capital is any resource that can be employed to produce value for its user.

There are three kinds of *life capital* we all have at our disposal:

- Personal capital (what you can do)
  - Time and abilities
  - Knowledge
  - Connections
- Purpose capital (what you've learned from your journey and experiences)

  - Journey-wisdom
  - Moral compass—values, beliefs, and spirituality
- Economic capital (available financial resources)
  - Income
  - Personal wealth
  - Family wealth

What if some of the goals you wish to pursue require more effort or ability than you yourself can provide? What if something, or several things, on your list will require the involvement of many other people?

What about money? How much will you need to accomplish everything on your success map? There is *never* enough money to do everything you want to do.

**Timing and Life Capital Requirements for Carl Nelson**

What are the most important measures of success for you right now and what of your life capital will you need to achieve them?

This step in the process organizes your success map around your priorities. Then you determine the timing for pursuing each metric. Finally, you ascertain what form or forms of your life capital will be needed to achieve each metric of success.

The Life Capital Resource Analysis for Carl Nelson is shown on the next page. Each metric of success identified in the vision phase of the success mapping process is listed on the grid. The list is then prioritized according to what is important to you. Carl's vision for success contains 51 measures. The first 11 of the 51 measures are illustrated in Figure 7.1.

**What This Means For You**

In this phase of the process, it isn't important to determine with great accuracy what the life capital requirements are for each metric of success. It is more important to identify which forms of life capital will be called on and when each metric will be pursued. Going through this process and then visually assessing the number of instances that each form of life capital will be needed to achieve success may cause you to adjust your priority ranking and/or timing of when you would pursue each metric of success.

## Figure 7.1 / Carl Nelson Life Capital Resource Analysis – 2015

| PRIORITY | | TIMING | | | PURPOSE CAPITAL | | PERSONAL CAPITAL | | | ECONOMIC CAPITAL | | |
|---|---|---|---|---|---|---|---|---|---|---|---|---|
| Ranking | | Want to do this Now | Want to do this later | Ongoing | Journey – Wisdom | Values / Beliefs | Knowledge | Time / Abilities | Connections | Personal Wealth | Family Wealth | Income |
| 1 | Vacation home in the Rockies | ✓ | | | *** | *** | * | *** | *** | | ***** | **** |
| 2 | Retire by year-end | ✓ | | | ***** | *** | *** | **** | **** | ***** | | |
| 3 | Be more involved with my church community | | | ∞ | *** | **** | * | * | * | | | ** |
| 4 | Management development plan | ✓ | | | ***** | ***** | ** | *** | ** | | *** | *** |
| 5 | Keynote speech at the Association's Annual Conference | ✓ | | | ** | ** | *** | * | * | | | ** |
| 6 | Anniversary trip June 2016 to Europe | ✓ | | | ** | *** | * | *** | ** | | | *** |
| 7 | Spousal Weekend personal growth retreat | | ✓ | | *** | *** | * | ** | * | | | ** |
| 8 | Establish annual distribution policy | ✓ | | | *** | ** | *** | * | *** | | **** | *** |
| 9 | Work with legal team on everyone's estate plans regarding the company | | ✓ | | *** | *** | **** | ** | ***** | | | **** |
| 10 | Long-range plan for business's ability to support the next 3 generations' interests | | ✓ | | **** | **** | ***** | ** | **** | | | *** |
| 11 | Update buy/sell agreement | ✓ | | | ***** | ***** | *** | * | ** | | | *** |

This phase of the process is intended to give you a 50,000-foot view of what will be needed to achieve each metric of success. The fine-tuning comes in the next phase of the process.

/ 8 /

# The Legacy Strategy

## SUSTAINING SUCCESS

The "how" of the success mapping process comes to life in the creation, implementation, and execution of the legacy strategy. This is the bridge to the practical side of how families can best manage their affairs to pursue what matters most.

In the previous step a life capital resource analysis was produced. As you look at this grid ask yourself, how can I use my limited resources to achieve every metric of success in pursuit of what matters most?

Since there are only 24 hours available each day how do you decide which of the many pursuits will be allocated any of those hours, especially if there are more hours needed than you have available? The same is true for all other forms of your life capital resources.

This phase of the process provides the mechanism and methodology for allocating your resources. While the visioning phase of the success mapping process encourages you to imagine what you would want in an unconstrained world, the strategy planning, implementation and execution phase guides you on how best to use the scarce resources of your constrained world.

The legacy strategy planning phase is often overlooked in most of the widely read literature on the subject of multi-generational family wealth because it is the most difficult to do. Yet preparing for generational transition is possibly the most important phase of the success mapping process. It's not enough to agree "We are family, here's why that matters, and we want our family to flourish for a very long time." How will that happen if no plan is in place to guide the family in the use of its resources?

Maintaining a sense of balance in the pursuit of each objective is important. If you spend all your time pursuing one metric of success, your overall result will be lopsided. A common example is the entrepreneur such as we saw in Bruce's story from the previous chapter who concentrates on establishing and expanding his business at the expense of time with his children. Finding balance among your pursuits is how you experience success across a wide range of measures.

Phil is a case in point.

**Family or Clients?**

Many years ago my friend Phil, a financial advisor, announced that he'd be taking three weeks off each quarter of the year to do something with his wife and/or his family. He talked about going on trips, working on projects with his kids and their families, enjoying leisure activities with his wife. He was setting aside four times a year to focus on his family.

This plan certainly sounded appealing. Just one little issue needed to be addressed before it could happen: Phil's clients needed help with their financial affairs whether he was in the office or not.

Phil set about analyzing what needed to be done to allow him to serve his clients and be with his family at the same time. The answer seems pretty obvious. Colleagues and staff would have to take care of his clients while he was away, and he would have to pay them to do so.

In this instance, two of the three forms of Phil's capital were involved as he pursued what mattered most to him. To free up his personal capital, his time, he had to use some of his economic capital, his money.

All forms of life capital are "scarce" in the sense that your needs and wants are greater than your ability to fulfill them. You don't have unlimited time, you don't have unlimited money, you don't know everything. Consequently, you must determine how you want to allocate your life capital in pursuit of what matters most to you. This allocation process can be haphazard or it can be planned.

**Needs, Wants, and Aspirations**

In 1952, economist Harry Markowitz introduced the world to Modern Portfolio Theory, a system to guide investors based on their preferences for risk and return.

Using this statistical approach, an investor theoretically would be able to invest in a portfolio of assets that would produce an expected return for an acceptable level of risk. The problem is that real-world investing rarely reflects theoretical expectations. Ask any investor how his portfolio has performed and the honest ones will tell you they never get what they expected.

More than 50 years later, Ashvin Chhabra published a seminal article[4]. In his theory, investors are acceptably irrational (Markowitz's theory assumed that all investors are rational). Chhabra contended that individuals' investment decisions are influenced by emotions. Their behavior therefore is irrational. Chhabra's model is based on a simplified version of psychologist Abraham Maslow's Hierarchy of Needs, which divides the motivation for human behavior into needs, wants, and aspirations.

In Chhabra's Maslovian model, people subdivide their wealth and investments into three emotional categories:

- Needs-based investments are expected to keep you safe regardless of how the rest of the investment world is performing: "I don't want to lose sleep at night."
- Wants-based investments are meant to finance your purchase of what you want by subjecting this money to the ups and downs of the financial markets: "I like driving a foreign sports car."
- Aspiration-based investments carry significant risk in an attempt to greatly improve your financial condition: "I want to create far more wealth than I have now."

We have expanded this methodology, which Chhabra furthered in a recent book, to think more broadly about each measure of suc-

4 Ashvin B. Chhabra, "Beyond Markowitz: A Comprehensive Wealth Allocation Framework for Individual Investors", *Journal of Wealth Management*, vol. 7, no. 4, Spring 2005, pp. 8–34.

cess as essential, important, or aspirational[5]. Looking at the family's measures of success through this prism, a family can allocate all forms of their life capital based on this framework.

Let's look at Carl Nelson's life capital resource analysis to understand how it works.

The ability to achieve expected outcomes is dependent on the probability of realizing each goal. The greater the probability of achieving a goal carries less uncertainty. Therefore the risk/reward trade-off will be low. The greater the uncertainty the higher the expected pay-off.

Carl was asked to categorize each of his measures of success based on its significance to the family in achieving that metric. I explained this is why it's important to start with the creation of the family mission statement because it provides the basis for determining each metric's position in the framework as essential, important, or aspirational.

Carl categorized his measures of success which were then sorted using the framework (see Figure 8.1 for an excerpt of his worksheet). I pointed out that items marked as essential are considered by him as non-negotiable. These items could not be compromised, they simply had to occur. Each of his essential goals would need the certainty that the forms of life capital required to meet these needs would not fail him.

Using life capital to pursue goals considered to be important carry a higher degree of uncertainty in being able to accomplish each of these goals because of the influence and impact of factors beyond the family's control.

Carl's highest priority and first to be rated as important was the vacation home in the Rocky Mountains. Weather, for example, could extend the construction schedule of the mountain property beyond an expected completion date that would've allowed them to be in the house for a special occasion or holiday. Or if Carl planned to use proceeds from some of his investments to pay for the construction of this home, a falling stock market could reduce the amount of money he has available to pursue this goal.

5 Chhabra, Ashvin B., *The Aspirational Investor*, New York, NY, HarperCollins, 2015

**Figure 8.1 / Carl Nelson Life Capital Allocation Framework – 2015**

| PRIORITY | | | TIMING | | | PURPOSE CAPITAL | | PERSONAL CAPITAL | | | ECONOMIC CAPITAL | | |
|---|---|---|---|---|---|---|---|---|---|---|---|---|---|
| Essential / Important / Aspirational | Ranking | | Want to do this Now | Want to do this later | Ongoing | Journey – Wisdom | Values / Beliefs | Knowledge | Time / Abilities | Connections | Personal Wealth | Family Wealth | Income |
| E | 2 | Retire by year-end | ✓ | | | ***** | *** | *** | **** | **** | ***** | | |
| E | 7 | Spousal Weekend personal growth retreat | | ✓ | | *** | *** | * | ** | * | | | ** |
| E | 9 | Work with legal team on everyone's estate plans regarding the company | | ✓ | | *** | *** | **** | ** | ***** | | | **** |
| I | 1 | Vacation home in the Rockies | ✓ | | | *** | *** | * | *** | *** | | ***** | **** |
| I | 3 | Be more involved with my church community | | | ∞ | *** | **** | * | * | * | | | ** |
| I | 4 | Management development plan | ✓ | | | ***** | ***** | ** | *** | ** | | *** | *** |
| A | 5 | Keynote speech at the Association's Annual Conference | ✓ | | | ** | ** | *** | * | * | | | ** |
| A | 8 | Establish annual distribution policy | ✓ | | | *** | ** | *** | * | *** | | **** | *** |
| A | 10 | Long-range plan for business's ability to support the next 3 generations' interests | | ✓ | | **** | **** | ***** | ** | **** | | | *** |

Finally, aspirational goals for Carl and his family are those that are most closely aligned with the family's ability to live its legacy and to perpetuate this legacy for future generations.

I told Carl he would most likely be working on a number of success measures at any given time. Some might be essential while others are important or aspirational. The key is to understand the significance of each metric of success as it reflects the family's values articulated in their family mission statement. In turn, he and his family would be able to use their life capital for what matters most.

### A Blueprint for Success

Every step of the success mapping process builds on what has come before. At this point, the success mapping process has all of the necessary ingredients to create the family's legacy strategy. The family has created a mission statement, articulated its vision for the future, and performed a values-based analysis of what will be needed to pursue what matters most.

Now a legacy strategy can be created for the family to implement and execute.

In the strategic planning phase a family will make decisions on how best to pursue what matters most. They will consider how to allocate their life capital resources in their endeavors.

The legacy strategy pulls everything together. It lays out the success map objectives based on their importance, what resources are needed to accomplish each objective, and the timing for action. The legacy strategy will also make it easier for your advisors to work together in helping you in your pursuits.

Properly executed, the legacy strategy will serve as the family's action plan to achieve what matters most.

The Winston family is a case in point.

### The Winston Family Meeting

Jeff and Melanie Winston and their family had been working through the success mapping process with Coppertree to create and implement their family legacy strategy. All six of their children, their children's spouses, and the grandchildren were able to attend the annual family meeting as a next step in the process. The objective of this meeting was to bring all of the previous work together.

Jeff and Melanie were a bit overwhelmed by the prospect of tackling everything the family had identified as measures of what a well-lived life meant to them. Where should they start and what would it take for them and their family to truly be successful in the way they envisioned?

With everyone assembled in the conference room Jeff began the meeting by saying that he and Melanie were proud of the effort the entire family made in getting them to this day. They were both pleased that their wealth would be something that the family today and future generations of their family could use and enjoy.

Jeff continued by telling the family that he and Melanie promised to work hard to help each of them find their own path. As he looked around the room, he said that all he could think of is how happy he was for his family.

The kids still weren't used to the buttoned-up father they had known being so openly emotional. But since the family started working on success mapping, Jeff was a new man. After years spent running hard with his head down as he grew the family's business, Winston Processing Inc., he was looking up and seeing the world around him. The awakening he had experienced during the success mapping process was a welcome change the whole family embraced.

Melanie then said it was time to put all of the work they'd done into action. She noted that each branch of the family spent time with Coppertree describing their journeys, dreaming about the possibilities, and expressing their wishes for what they wanted for themselves and their families. To Melanie, it seemed a little daunting to think they could actually achieve what's important to everyone. She expressed her confidence that there would be a way to make it happen with their advisors' help.

Jeff added that he spent his entire life focused on his own successes that he measured in terms of financial and business achievements. Now he was ready to share and use his successes to pursue what was important to his entire family.

Jeff told everyone their opinion mattered and that he wanted each of them to actively participate and contribute to the conversation they were about to have regarding their future. Now the Winston's would actually get to work on what they wanted to accomplish. Family members were encouraged to offer their thoughts and comments on what they were about to do.

We uncovered the wall to reveal the Winston family's Success Map (see Figure 8.2 for an excerpt of the Winston family's Success Map). There, in front of everyone, was everything they had talked about, brought together into a highly intricate and detailed summary of what was important to the family.

I asked everyone to take a look at the first pieces of information: the *essentials*. I said these are the measures of success the family considers fundamental.

Jeff spoke up saying this was the challenge that he saw. There's so much he wanted to do; so much he wanted the family to do. And that he wanted it all! The scope of the family's vision for what they wanted and what would be needed to achieve it seemed impossibly vast. This represented where they want to go and the importance of each stop along the way.

Then I explained the next phase of the process would establish the work plan, the *how* of getting there. It would help them figure out the route to take, how fast they would need to go, and what risks or constraints they might be faced with along the way.

One of the children commented they were also interested in some of the items that were characterized as *important* or *aspirational*. She wanted to know when they would get to those ideas. She was really interested in career development for family members. She pointed out that that was all the way down in the *important* section on the poster and it wasn't even the highest-ranking item. She asked if it mattered where they started if they're all important.

I said everything on this framework was important or it wouldn't have been on the framework. Her question illustrated the challenge that lay before the family: Where *do* you start?

The answer is, wherever you want. Some of what's on the framework will be more important to a daughter than it might be to her brother. Maybe he wants to lead the way on establishing a distri-

**Figure 8.2 / Winston Family Success Map**

| | Priority Rank | Measures of Success | Champion | Stakeholder | Focus |
|---|---|---|---|---|---|
| ESSENTIAL | 1 | Estate plan updates | Each Household | Family | Legacy |
| | 2 | Education plan for grandkids | Jeff/Melanie | Family | Goals |
| | 3 | European barge cruise | Jeff/Melanie | Self | Enjoyment |
| | 4 | Weekly email to the grandkids about my childhood | Jeff | Self | Legacy |
| | 5 | Stories of the early days of our marriage | Jeff/Melanie | Family | Legacy |
| | 6 | Take grandkids to volunteer at soup kitchen | Jeff | Self | Impact |
| | 7 | Annual trip to Sea Island | Whole Family | Family | Enjoyment |
| IMPORTANT | 1 | Update the Family Continuity Plan | Family Council | Family | Legacy |
| | 2 | Establish annual distribution policy | Family Council & WPI Board | Our Enterprise | Goals |
| | 3 | Add new Ferrari to car collection | Jeff | Self | Enjoyment |
| | 4 | Finish grad school | Melanie | Self | Goals |
| | 5 | Dinner with the board | Family Council | Our Enterprise | Goals |
| | 6 | Anniversary trip June 2016 to Europe | Jeff and Melanie | Self | Enjoyment |
| | 7 | Career development for family members | Family Council | Our Enterprise | Impact |
| ASPIRATIONAL | 1 | G-3 Mission Statement | Family Council | Family | Legacy |
| | 2 | Long-range strategic plan for WPI | WPI Leadership Team | Family | Goals |
| | 3 | Art museum renovation | Melanie | Community | Legacy |
| | 4 | New ventures | Board and Family Council | Our Enterprise | Goals |
| | 5 | Foundation grant review process | Family Council | Community | Impact |

bution plan from the business; maybe his sister wants to focus on working with the art museum to fund the renovation of the museum. Each family member has their personal time and abilities that can be employed in pursuing the goals listed. This is an important aspect to carrying out a legacy strategy as a family. Individual family members could allocate their resources to different pursuits.

This is oftentimes a different way of thinking about what it takes to get things done for the original wealth creator, especially successful business owners. They've always used their business mind to evaluate decisions that needed to be made. As the leader of their business they direct what everyone was to do and how they were to use the assets of the company like machinery and trucks to achieve their goals. It was their company and as such were entitled to do what they wanted. And as long as everyone did what they were told, everything got done the way they wanted it to.

Frequently, this is how these individuals function at home as well. As this new thought sinks in, they recognize their family doesn't need to be told what to do, especially in the context of how best to use the family's life capital. Money and power are not the levers of control in the family environment because that doesn't honor what most families view as a healthy relationship built on transparency, communication, and trust.

A life well-lived was now more real for the Winstons than it ever was before.

Something very special happened as this family began to see themselves in this new light. Yet this something was unconsciously there all along. It just needed the right moment to become a part of the family's conscious lives. Taking these steps builds a high degree of trust and respect.

I continued by asking them how were they possibly going to get everything done on this list. I then simply said they would proceed one step at a time.

One of the kids spoke up saying that each of them could take their own steps, so to speak. He asked me if this is what I was suggesting.

I said that's the beauty of this process. There really is a lot to do here and no single individual—not even the original wealth creator—can do it alone. You've heard the saying 'It takes a village to raise a child'? In the context of our work, I would suggest it takes a family to perpetuate a legacy.

### The Legacy Strategy

This wonderful tapestry of measures that families articulate as their vision of success will come to life through the efforts of everyone involved in the process. It will take teamwork to make it happen. Some family members will work on one metric while a few more might work on something else. Collectively, their dream comes alive.

What is done at this point is to develop the legacy strategy to pursue the family's vision of success. I would suggest that you look at this in blocks of time you can apportion toward getting what you want. The most common interval is a year. So this would become an annual strategy for you and your family. It would break down the year in monthly segments, with each month focusing on one or more considerations. The strategy would also define the who, what, where, why, and how necessary to accomplish your objectives.

Going forward, this process should be repeated annually. This becomes the primary role of a family council. This is the leadership forum for your family and should provide the mechanism to ensure that you stay on track. For the families we serve, we work with the family council in this regard.

An excerpt from the Winston family legacy strategy follows:

---

**Winston Family Legacy Strategy**

We, the Winston family, have created this family legacy strategy and plan to help us pursue what matters most to us. Through the development of success maps for each household of the family and an assessment of how the family's capital was deployed, a legacy strategy and plan has been designed for the coming year to improve our chances of achieving the goals we have set forth.

There are four strategic objectives we have agreed to pursue next year:

1. Develop a business plan for Winston Processing Inc. (WPI) that produces a level of profits to support family distributions of at least $1.2 million next year.
   - Determine the family's commitment to the growth and success of the business for the next five years.

- Review and assess the company's historic results and forecast future results based on management's strategic direction.
- Conduct financial analysis using pro-forma financials to determine the feasibility of a $1.2 million distribution to the family next year.

2. Implement an investment program for the Winston Family LLC Investment Partnership that will support a spending policy of 3% (after-tax, after-cost), with principle growth of 3% net of costs and distributions.
   - Complete financial needs audit and wealth allocation analysis.
   - Evaluate the current investment program's ability to meet the family's financial needs.
   - Ascertain the appropriate actions necessary to adjust the investment policy to reflect the family's growth and income strategy.
3. Issue grants and outright gifts of $1 million from the Winston Family Foundation.
   - Review and select grant requests to be funded.
   - Identify nonprofit organizations for annual gifting and determine size and timing of gifts.
4. Develop a program to be presented at the next Family Gathering to educate all family members on our roles and responsibilities in executing our multigenerational strategy for family resource stewardship.
   - Conduct research and analysis to project the potential needs of the family for at least the next two generations.
   - Establish wealth creation goals and wealth transition plans for successor generations.
   - Establish a family stewardship committee to manage the plan.

The family will work with our advisors, who will assist in the execution of this plan. The family will look to our advisors for insight, analysis, and recommendations with regard to the family's progress in pursuing the objectives outlined above. Our advisors will also work with the individual members of the family in their pursuit of what matters most to them, based on their personal definition of success.

The Family Council has been charged with the duty of monitoring progress of the plan and will keep the family informed throughout the year. The family intends to update the plan annually.

**Methodology**

The first steps in pursuing the coming year's goals are to establish a baseline for each of this year's objectives. This should be followed by the creation of action plans and measures for each goal.

***Objective # 1: Family Distribution***

The focus of Winston Manufacturing (WPI) for the past few years has been on incremental growth in the current economic climate. Company management was charged with producing results that covered the cost of capital for the organization. The company is projected to generate a return on capital of 17% for the current year. This is greater that the weighted average cost of capital of 11% for the firm.

The family believes that the business should be generating profits greater than our cost of capital to justify a family distribution. Looking at company results and the current economic conditions, we have decided that a family distribution is appropriate for this year. We have determined that we plan to withdraw $1.2 million this year.

As in years past, the family's philosophy is to share 10% of the firm's profits in the form of bonuses with WPI's employees. A profit-sharing bonus will be distributed to all employees at the next quarterly employee meeting.

***Objective # 2: Growth and Income Plan for the Family LLC***

The performance of the family LLC, like WPI, is subject to current economic conditions. The investment strategy in place before the recession of 2008–2009 did not protect the family from the risk of income loss. Furthermore, the need for income pushed the portfolio managers to overreact to portfolio volatility associated with growth-oriented investments, resulting in ill-timed liquidations and missed opportunities.

Looking ahead, the family has determined that the investment program should be restructured using a goals-based investment strategy. Simply put, the family wishes to receive periodic distributions from the LLC and also expects that the value of the LLC will grow sufficiently to maintain the buying power of the portfolio across time.

The family has decided to establish three separate capital allocations: a cash-flow-generating allocation; an allocation to maintain buying power through modest risk/growth-oriented investments; and an allocation for new wealth-creating family ventures or private equity opportunities. Using this methodology, the family expects to minimize the opposing risks associated with investments designed to address a spending policy versus investments that are intended to satisfy growth strategies. The family views the family business as a component of its aspirational wealth-creating mechanism. New wealth-creation ventures will be reviewed and considered by the family as circumstances arise.

The goal of the safety portfolio is to generate an annual cash flow to the family of at least $1.5 million adjusted for inflation. The portfolio will retain 5 years of cash flow or $7.5 million to be invested in non-risk bearing investments. The family considers earned income from professional and career pursuits as a component of the income portfolio. Therefore, total cash flow to the family is expected to be significantly greater than the return on the safety portfolio itself.

The goal of the market portfolio is to replenish the safety portfolio every 5 years with $7.5 million (adjusted for inflation). The first $37.5 million of this portfolio is allocated to the funding of this goal. The remaining assets of the market portfolio are expected to produce market returns that can be used in support of the family's lifestyle needs.

***Objective # 3: Foundation Management***

The family has determined that a total of $1 million in distributions from the family foundation is appropriate for the year. The family has decided to use 75% of this distribution toward grant requests, with the remaining 25% distributed as gifts to organizations that have exemplified the virtues of getting a good education as a means of achieving financial independence.

Family members wishing to present candidates for grants and gifts must be actively involved with the organization in a leadership position, such as serving on the board. Unsolicited requests will be accepted only from organizations whose mission and vision are in line with the mission and vision of the foundation.

***Objective # 4: Family Stewardship Program***

During the next Family Assembly and Family Reunion (Annual Family Meeting), a program is to be presented as a series of age-specific workshops to educate all members of the family on the importance of serving as a steward for the family's legacy. The most important consideration is to maintain family unity for many years to come. This can only happen if the family understands the family's journey: where it has come from, where it is today, and where it wants to be in the future.

The stewardship program is intended to educate family members about the importance of stewarding our wealth beyond the family's present needs, especially if the goal of the family is for future generations to be able to enjoy the quality of life the family is experiencing today. Concepts of wealth creation and prudent decision-making will be introduced to help family members understand how to balance the needs of present generations of the family with those of future generations.

A stewardship strategy will be created to guide the family in addressing their responsibilities toward the perpetuation of the family and its legacy.

**Timing**

The family will work with our advisors in the implementation and execution of the plan. Our lead advisor will present a proposed schedule of activities, meetings, and gatherings to assist the family in pursuing the plan's objectives.

In addition to executing the legacy strategy, the family may work with our advisors to address the family annual personal business affairs schedule. The monthly schedule is designed to balance the time-sensitive affairs such as tax compliance with time-neutral considerations such as a review of the family balance sheet or wealth transition planning meetings.

The next step is to create a master calendar of events, combining the issues of the strategic plan and the family business affairs schedule. The advisory team will provide a master calendar and individual family member calendars highlighting activities and meetings relevant to each member's responsibilities.

**Value**

The family recognizes that this system of planning and decision-making will greatly enhance the probability that the family's legacy will flourish well into the future.

**Conclusion**

The annual legacy strategy document will serve as a guide and benchmark for the family's progress during the project period. The strategy will be monitored, assessed, and adjusted as necessary throughout the implementation of the action steps to ensure that it reflects the family's interests and their pursuit of what matters most to them.

### What This Means For You

In Part Two and Three of the book you learned how to use the success mapping process. The end result gives you and your family a strategy for pursuing what matters most as you live your lasting legacy.

You can have it all. You just can't have it all at once. Using the success mapping process you can strategically prioritize your goals and allocate your resources to pursue what matters based on your values and your dreams for today and beyond.

Part Four will look at some important issues to consider in living your legacy.

/ PART FOUR /

# Challenges of Succession

/ 9 /

# Succession

## SECURING YOUR FUTURE

For families with wealth from a multigenerational enterprise, succession involves not just estate planning or tax planning but a plan for perpetuating the family legacy itself.

The succession phase of success mapping focuses on managing the interplay of money, power, and relationships. All three require individual attention as well as attention to the interaction between them.

Issues relating to the transition of the management of the family enterprise—the money machine—are traditionally considered in business succession planning. But succession also entails the transition of ownership (power), and educating the next generation of family members on how to get along in their efforts to perpetuate the family legacy (relationships).

My own family experience serves as a good example of how each of these components of succession can play out within a family.

### Management Transition

When Dad opened the doors to his tool & die shop in 1972, I worked for him in the summers doing odd jobs: sweeping the floor (although the family joke is he would frequently tell me I was doing it all wrong), cleaning machines, driving the delivery truck, getting lunch for the guys.

Occasionally, I would ask Dad why he started the business, and what the business meant to him. These questions drove him nuts. (He and I are exact opposites on the Myers-Briggs personality type indicator, by the way. I'm an I-N-F-P; he's an E-S-T-J—essentially we're from different planets!) He said it didn't matter what the business meant to him—all he was doing was creating a job for himself that would pay him a little more money than if he worked for someone else. He went on to say that it was also a job for me, my brother Mike, and my sister Lynn, if we were interested in going to work there.

Mike started working for Dad's company while he was still in high school and decided early on that he wanted to make his career there. Since Dad's plan on retiring was to turn the management of the business over to any of his children who worked there, Mike's leadership training began the day he walked through the doors of the shop. It was experiential rather than formal. Mike learned from what he observed day by day.

Dad wasn't much for academic training, especially when it came to the highly skilled expertise of the company's toolmakers. Unless you had actually done it yourself, it would be a challenge to understand the unique issues that arose in manufacturing production dies and specialty machines. So Mike moved up through the ranks, from floor sweeper (where we all started!) to toolmaker to foreman. After Mike turned 40 he started meeting with Dad regularly to talk about running the manufacturing and operations of the business.

Dad was reluctant to bring in professional managers to help him run the business of the company. Instead, he chose to manage it himself, with some help from a few trusted advisors. Dad was known for the never-ending stream of questions he would ask these outside advisors as he was trying to discern the best course of action when faced with complex business decisions.

Mike was asked to sit in on Dad's meetings with the outside advisors to see how Dad drew on their expertise. Dad was patient but relentless in questioning his advisors. He could afford to play 20 Questions with his advisors because he had Mike running the manufacturing operations of the business and didn't need to allocate any of his own time to that task.

Over the final five years of Dad's leadership, Mike learned a considerable amount about running the business of the company as he sat in on these meetings. And in 2008–2009 he experienced firsthand what it's like to ride out a serious economic downturn. All of this, in Dad's mind, prepared Mike to take over the business.

Then, without any prior indication, Dad announced in November 2010 at the age of 76 that he was ready to retire at the end of the year. And he did just that, confident that Mike was ready to succeed him. Mike willingly assumed the role of president in January 2011.

Since then, Mike has put a board of advisors in place and is constantly looking for opportunities to learn and grow. He has been investing time in leadership and management training courses. Mike continues to attend workshops, conferences, and other educational programs for business leaders and managers in an effort to improve his ability to lead the family business forward.

I should also mention that my sister Lynn has been employed in the business for close to 20 years. Dad asked her to be Mike's right-hand person and to manage all aspects of the business that Mike either didn't want to or couldn't manage due to any number of factors. We kiddingly refer to Lynn as the CEMDNWTDO (Chief Everything Mike Does Not Want to Do Officer). She's very good at it! She oversees finance, marketing, IT, and HR.

Since Dad's retirement, the business has grown by more than 50 percent from its post-recession low, with record revenues and profits in the most recent fiscal year. Prospects for the next several years are quite promising. Mike was ready (with Lynn by his side), the company was ready, and Mom and Dad are enjoying their golden years.

As the family thinks about the future, it's time to look for the next generation of family business leaders. No one in the grandkid generation has been working there since high school like Mike did. Mike's oldest child, Beth, is now working at the firm full-time on the corporate side, but it's too early to tell what her role may be in the future. She has been a wonderful addition and continues the tradition of FC Industries being a family business. Other grandkids have indicated they may be interested in running the business someday. Until then, the family will need a Plan B.

Mike, Lynn, and I have talked about the possibility of bringing in a professional manager to succeed Mike until an interested grandkid—if there is one—is ready and qualified to step into the leadership role. Regardless of who Mike's successor will ultimately be, the family has begun working on formalizing a management succession plan in anticipation of Mike's eventual retirement in roughly 10 years.

Management succession planning is an ongoing process. The sooner you begin this process, the better your chances of successfully navigating it. The best CEOs begin looking for their replacement the first day they are on the job!

Dad's strategy for the future was typical of many succession plans for family-owned businesses. Succession is usually thought of as a management transition issue. His concerns were straightforward: Make sure I have enough money and turn over the helm to my successor while the ship is afloat. There was never a mention of who owned the boat. For him, ownership didn't matter. The boat only had meaning to the crew who worked on it.

But when the boat keeps getting bigger, its future owners are eventually going to want to know what's in it for them. For multigenerational families who own a business, succession means more than planning for the next leader of the business. It means planning for the next generation of owners.

**Ownership Succession**

When you start a business all that matters is to make more money than you're spending. Maybe you invest some of your money (if you have any) in equipment you need. Or you might be lucky enough to be able to use other people's money to fund the start-up of your business.

As the founder of the business, you aren't as concerned about the return on the money you or other people have invested. All you think about is making more than you're spending. You think about the income statement, nonstop.

Someday, the balance sheet may give you anxiety attacks when you eventually start thinking about the need to repay anyone who gave you money to start your business. But not today. You've just begun and you're full of optimism and terror at the same time. You're an entrepreneur! So you don't think about the balance sheet ... for now.

My father's simple, straightforward, and highly successful philosophy focused on his business's income statement. Once when I asked him whether he had a business plan, he snapped: "Pay the bank, pay my suppliers, and pay my employees, of which I am one." Beyond that, he had no other stakeholders to consider, especially not himself as owner. He got what the business could give him in the form of a paycheck. What more did he need?

Capital at risk? Meaningless. The line item on the balance sheet that represented his "worth" in the company was nothing more than a placeholder to make the balance sheet come out right. It didn't really mean anything to him until I started asking more questions. "Dad, what about the grandkids? Our wealth transition plans pass ownership to each successive generation. What happens once the grandkids are the owners of the business and start asking what's in it for them?"

Like it or not, at some point an owner of Dad's business is going to have expectations about the "money" he or she has in it. I remember the day when this finally started to make some sense to Dad.

A few years before Dad retired, I met with him, my brother Mike, the company controller, and Dad's accountant to discuss the future of the business from an estate-planning standpoint. I passed out a copy of the balance sheet with the Total Shareholders' Equity line circled. Without any explanation, I asked each of them what they felt a fair return would be if they were investing in the stock market.

I started with the accountant. His expectation was the lowest. He said a 6 percent return was all he would need. The controller said 7. My brother said 10. And then I asked Dad, "What do you think is a fair return for a stock market portfolio?" His answer: 12 percent.

These answers didn't surprise me. The more conservative accountant and controller would be satisfied with a return slightly higher than they would have received had they invested in 10-year U.S. Treasury bonds (I consider this to be the risk-free-investment benchmark).

Mike, having spent a lifetime working closely with our father, was a little more risky in his expected return. The real entrepreneur in the room had the highest return expectation and thus the greatest appetite for and comfort with risk.

Why did he give such a high number relative to everyone else's? I asked Dad. He said that if he was going to risk his money in the stock market, then he expected a return sufficient to offset that risk. I then asked him if he would expect that kind of return on all his investments.

He looked at me quizzically. "All of my investments are in the stock and bond markets." What about his investment in FC Industries? He said he didn't have an expectation of a return because he didn't really feel like he had any money "invested" in the company. Then I pointed to the number I had circled. "What about this number here, Dad?"

He said that number—a large one—didn't really mean anything to him. "If you decided to sell the company," I persisted, "and you actually got a check equal to shareholders' equity, what would your return expectation be on this money if you invested it in the stock market?" Once again he said 12 percent.

I pointed out to him that shareholders' equity was his real money. It was the value of his money that was invested in the business. I also explained that the returns on this money should be treated and viewed no differently from returns on any of his other investments.

In fact, I said, he should have a *higher* expectation for returns on this money. In theory, this money was invested in a significantly riskier venture with far greater uncertainty and far less liquidity; given these additional risks, he should expect a higher return.

He looked at me and said there was no way the company would be able to generate that kind of return on "his" money. To his surprise, I walked him through a calculation that measured the return the business had actually generated on his investment during the previous year. It was significantly greater than 12 percent.

Dad shook his head. "I don't see how I can expect anything from the company beyond my paycheck."

I pointed out that he chose to reinvest all the profit generated on his capital back into the company to provide growth capital for the business, when he could have chosen to take some of this money for himself. "The company wouldn't have been able to grow as big as it did if you hadn't reinvested your profits back into the business. But," I said, "it doesn't have to be this way forever. The company might not need all of the owners' profits to be plowed back into the business in the future. At what point is the company big enough? Is there a size we want it to be, in terms of total sales, total profits, or a combination of various metrics? This," I concluded, "is the issue for the next generation that will need to be addressed."

Dad knew where I was going with this and responded that there just wasn't enough money coming out of the business to give all the owners a check. I suggested that this was at the heart of the very issue we needed to prepare for before the business passed to the grandkids.

For the first time, Dad paused and his gaze went off into the distance. "This is what scares me to death. There is no way this business can support all nine grandchildren. I don't even think we could employ all nine of them if they wanted to work there. I worry about what this will do to them."

I reminded him that our ownership transition plan called for the grandchildren to eventually own the business after he, Mom, Mike, Lynn, and I were no longer alive. He expressed again his worry that the grandkids would fight among themselves if they weren't all getting the same benefit from the company.

Then he said something that has provided our family with the "why" that we use to guide our decisions as a family as we think about FC Industries. He said, "More than anything, I want for all of you—you, Mike and Lynn, and the grandkids—to be together. I want family harmony."

I then asked, "What should the grandkids do if the business was causing a fight?"

"Sell it."

"Sell the business?"

"Yes. If the business gets in the way of our family staying together, it should be sold."

For the first time, we now had articulated, as a family, what was important to us: unity and harmony. We end our family council meetings and annual family meetings by asking ourselves how we did with respect to promoting unity and harmony within our family for generations to come. If we in any way detracted from being together and in harmony, then we all agree to address whatever issue caused this problem at our next gathering.

### Preparing for the G-3 Transition

Years earlier, as Dad was grappling with the issues of ownership transition, he expressed reluctance about giving non-leaders a say in how the business was operated. At the suggestion of his legal counsel, he decided to create two classes of ownership. One class had a vote, the other did not.

When it became clear that Mike was to succeed Dad as president of the company, the ownership interests were gifted to Mike, Lynn, and me. Mike was to receive the voting interests, while Lynn and I received an equal number of non-voting interests. This fulfilled Dad's objective of giving Mike the power to control the business. Lynn and I were merely along for the ride as owners without the authority to legally overrule Mike. Lynn and I were quite fine with this.

Dad chose Mike to be his management successor because of his tenure and his manufacturing expertise. As a family we were fortunate not to have any conflict between Mike and Lynn surrounding management succession. We want to ensure that succession to the next generation goes as smoothly. This is a current topic in our family council and annual family meeting discussions and will continue to play out into the future.

Lynn and I do have the power to sell our interests, and in that sense we can decide not to participate in the direction Mike chooses to take the company. As Mike, Lynn, and I thought about the future of the *power* aspect of the enterprise, we came to the decision that it would be best to convert to a single class of voting interests as we transitioned the ownership of the business to the next generation.

Mike has all of the controlling interests in the company, so he didn't have to do this, but because we all share our parents' desire for family harmony and unity, he concluded that having only his heirs controlling the company would be detrimental. I am grateful that Mike made this decision that will go a long way in perpetuating the legacy of our family.

As we hand off ownership and control of the business to the grandkids, or G-3 generation, the money machine will have to pay more attention to this new breed of stakeholder, the G-3 owners. The money machine will need to keep the power stakeholders satisfied. As owners, the G-3s will want to be informed about and pleased with the business's performance.

Families primarily grow through marriages and births. Education of these new members about the family's legacy and its enterprise assets is vital. Families must do all they can to minimize the disastrous effects of ignorance in making decisions pertaining to multigenerational legacy assets. Education is the key to overcoming ignorance.

### Final Thoughts

Whose dream are you living? Dad always told us when we were growing up that we could join the business. We could become a part of his dream. I chose not to join the company as a tool maker and instead went off to pursue my own dreams. I know this disappointed my father but he also supported me in doing what I wanted to do.

This is not always the case in some families. While we are a part of the family we are also individuals. Families need to respect that the values of each individual family member and those values of the family itself may or may not be one in the same. These are the families who are functioning at a higher level by accepting that we have personal identities along with our family identity.

I am thankful that Dad invited me back in to be a part of his dream through the work we've done at Coppertree for our family. He didn't have to do that. Yet his belief was, is, and will always be that we are striving to be a family living in harmony. Welcoming me back to participate in his dream of our family will be together for a very long time certainly is a testimony to his humility and willingness to do what it takes to make his dream a reality.

---

**Jenny's View: Who Am I?**

We are initially impacted by the family into which we are born. It is our first experience with a group of people who operate from standards formed by past experiences, relationships, cultural events and many other factors. The way we interact with the outside world is largely shaped by what we have learned from our parents and from other multigenerational forces. Our identity and behavior are shaped by our family of origin. As we grow and venture into the world outside the family, we maneuver through other systems such as school, employment, and social circles. Each has its own codes and standards.

The process of becoming a person who is able to function as part of a family or business system, without becoming absorbed by it, is also part of figuring out who you are and what is important to you. You are defining yourself. Think of the newly minted high school graduate sprinting off to her first year of college. How she adapts depends on how grounded she is in her knowledge of herself. If she has thought about what's important to her, what she will and will not do in certain situations, she will more likely be prepared to be a part of her new system without being swallowed up by it.

Thoughtfully acquired principles help guide decision-making about important family and social issues, leaving us less at the mercy of the emotions of the moment. What we say matches what we do.

People who haven't taken the time to understand and act on their core values often have an unrealistic dependency on the family or business that they're part of. Instead of developing their own beliefs through experience and reflection, they tend to adopt the general principles of the family or the organization. This kind of absorption into whatever system a person finds herself in can become comfortable. As long as the players are playing the role they've been taught, everybody gets along and the system functions well.

Independently functioning individuals have asked themselves questions such as:

- What kind of spouse, daughter, sister, and employee do I want to be?
- What do I need to do on an everyday basis to achieve that?
- What are my five core values that I can use to become my own person?
- What issues, situations, topics am I willing to take a stand on?
- What issues, situations, topics am I willing to compromise on?
- Am I able to take in other people's opinions without absorbing them?
- How do I manage myself in times of stress or anxiety while still maintaining my core beliefs?

How does a family make the tough decisions without causing stress? How do we all get along? These are questions we are often asked. Every family system or family business has its leaders, followers, and people in between. As a result, the families and individual members differ in the intensity of their emotional interdependence. The more intense the interdependence of the family, the less capacity they have to adapt to potentially stressful events.

Carla is a case in point

Carla, the only daughter of a devoutly religious couple, meets a young man, falls in love, and after years of dating they plan to announce their engagement. They have discussed the fact that Carla's fiancé didn't share her parents' religion and the parents don't approve. The young couple understand the reaction they may encounter when they break the news. After many conversations and deep soul searching, however, they decide that they'll put their relationship first. They will also respect Carla's parents' reaction, whatever it is, and keep the door open to them and welcome them in their lives. As the couple feared, the news of the engagement was not well received. Carla's parents threatened to disown her, to not attend to the wedding, and other consequences if she went through with her plan. This was very hurtful to Carla, but she went through with the wedding.

Carla's parents did not attend the wedding, but after a year and a half they began to understand that Carla was leading her life and if they wanted to be a part of it, they had to accept her husband. It took some time, but in the process Carla took a stand while at the same time stayed connected to her parents. They eventually did accept her husband into the family.

When someone changes her role as previously defined, the system usually responds negatively, pressuring the person to remain in her assigned role by issuing threats of punishment. A person who is able to withstand that pressure and clearly communicates her thoughts has a better chance of eventually being understood and accepted. In the process, she has established her new role, stated her beliefs, and acted on them while still remaining a part of the system.

How does a family make tough decisions without causing stress? How do we all get along? These are questions we are often asked. Families and their individual members differ in the intensity of their emotional interdependence. The more intense the interdependence, the less capacity family members have to adapt to potentially stressful events.

Everyone is subject to problems in his work and personal life, but less differentiated people and families are more vulnerable to periods of high stress. Instead of approaching a decision or any change such as succession, death, company restructuring, divorce with emotion, a less interdependent family would be more likely to look at the facts behind their choices, listen effectively to each member, and make a rational decision based on fact, not emotion.

### What This Mean For You

Succession is more than determining and transitioning to the next leader of the business. It also considers the next owners of the business as well. Preparing and positioning successors for each transition is vital to achieving a successful outcome.

What happens when ignorance rules the transition process?

/ 10 /

# Preparing and Positioning the Next Generation

According to an old saying, "Ignorance is bliss." For families seeking to live multi-generational legacies that last, ignorance may not be bliss. What happens when significant gaps in knowledge and awareness exist? My own experiences with Mary's family business are a case in point.

Mary and I married young. I was just shy of my 24th birthday; she was 23. About a year later we were at Mary's parents' house for Sunday dinner when my father-in-law asked me to come with him to another room so he could talk to me privately about the family business Mary's grandfather had founded back in 1919.

Mary's dad handed me a check that was made out to her, along with some kind of tax form. He said he'd been taking care of filing Mary's tax returns and now that she was married it was our responsibility. The check was a distribution from the family business that was to be used to pay income tax Mary owed for her ownership in it, plus a little extra that Mary's dad would deposit into a savings account he had set up for her.

I hadn't realized Mary was actually an owner of her grandfather's business. I knew her family owned it, but it never occurred to me that that meant Mary was an owner. So as I understood it, Mary would get money from her business but she couldn't keep much of it. What was the purpose of owning something that doesn't do anything for you except force you to pay taxes on income you never get to use? It was all a mystery to me. I'd been a biology major; I was working as a poorly paid salesman; I was only 25—what did I know about the language of business and finance? Even though my father had his own business, he hadn't taught me the lingo.

After we got home I asked Mary what she knew about the family business. "Not much," she replied. I also asked her about the savings account her dad had mentioned to me.

All she knew was that he would have her endorse checks like the one he gave me that evening, then he'd put the money in a savings account and use most of it to pay her income tax bill. "Any idea how much is in that account?" I asked. Her answer surprised me. It was a considerable sum.

My first thought was, "We sure could use this money!" Mary and I dreamed of buying a house before our first child was born. I suggested using her savings account for the down payment. She agreed.

Not long after, we found a lovely Cape Cod in a quiet neighborhood. We fell in love with it and put in an offer. We used the balance in her savings account to make the down payment and moved in one month before Katie was born.

It was an exciting time in our life. It was also a time of mounting curiosity for me with regard to Mary's family's business. What else was there to know about being owners?

The first thing I learned was that "we" were not owners; Mary was the owner through gifts of shares from her mother. I also learned that information about the business was not readily available to me or anyone else marrying 3rd generation family members.

I asked Mary to ask her dad if he would tell us anything more about her ownership. Let me be clear. I married into a wonderful, loving family and have had a great relationship with them since Day 1. But when it came to asking questions about the business, the family's philosophy was to share minimal information with non-owners, i.e. spouses.

Understandably, many family business owners worry about the possibility of in-laws' harming the business through greed or ignorance. Whether it's expecting more distributions or taking a job with the family firm only to disrupt it in some way, the risk of destructive change is something some families guard against by keeping information close to the vest.

But over the years I've served Coppertree's clients, including my own family, I've learned the real risk to the business and to the family is to keep everything secret. The less people know, the thinking goes, the less they can mess things up. But the truth is just the opposite. What you don't know can kill you.

**Transparency, Communication, Education**

To minimize the potential for misunderstandings and worse, it's vitally important to be transparent and to communicate with the entire family about what's going on in the family business. It's also important to educate new family members about the business.

If a new in-law member lacks knowledge about business principles, it is essential to teach him or her the basics at a minimum. This would include a fundamental understanding of how to read and interpret financial statements. Ignorance breeds chaos and bad decisions.

When Mary asked her dad whether he'd tell me about the business, she got the impression I shouldn't be poking my nose in. He was simply operating from the mind-set of sharing as little information about the business as possible with "outsiders."

I was bewildered. My wife owned something, but I wasn't supposed to ask questions about it? Maybe it would be better for her to get out of the business.

I decided it was time to take matters into my own hands. Our accountant informed me what Mary's ownership in the businesses was worth. It was a very substantial sum. The accountant walked us through the tax form and highlighted the line that represented her share of the profits for the previous year.

He also explained that since we were receiving only enough of the profits to pay the taxes, the remainder of her share of the profits was being reinvested in the business. Did this money have to go back into the business? He said no—all of the profits could be distributed to the owners. Mary and I looked at each other as the significance of this possibility sank in.

Driving home, we talked about what we had learned. We could put this money to any number of uses. We could fix up our house, buy a new car, go on trips. All we needed was to submit her redemption request to sell her interests back to the company. Why should her profits be used to expand the business? Didn't Mary have a say in how her money was being used? Shouldn't she get what was coming to her?

Many of the concerns Mary's family had about what might happen when newcomers learned there was a *money machine* came true, even though I had no intention of doing any harm to Mary or her family. I just wanted her to get what I thought was due her. I didn't understand why some of her money should stay in the company rather than be paid out to her.

I was an uneducated in-law on two fronts. First, as I've noted, I didn't understand the language of business. Second, I was never informed about the family's expectations, opportunities, and responsibilities for each of the owners and their spouses (me). I didn't know why the business existed and what it meant for Mary and the rest of the family co-owners.

Most of the decisions we made toward Mary's family business in those early years of our marriage were the result of ignorance. Of course, even educated decisions can be bad ones. But at least an educated decision-maker is aware of ramifications and consequences.

Family meetings are an excellent venue for informing new family members about the family business. They're also a wonderful forum for general business education, as well as a time to learn about family dynamics and the role they can play in making joint decisions.

Transparency is important, too. Secrecy breeds doubt. Education and transparency allow for informed decisions based on trust that those in charge are acting in the best interest of all involved.

The most successful multigenerational business-owning families I know have a structured and purposeful education program in place. What does a good education plan entail?

First and foremost, it informs family members why the business exists in the first place. History matters. If a family is fortunate enough to have the founder of the business still around to describe why and how he created it, this can be a very powerful basis for making decisions on behalf of the family and the business.

If Mary's grandfather were alive today, he might communicate with the family about how he saw his business as an economic resource to provide for his children and beyond. He might also talk about how the business could keep the family together. Decisions could then be made to support this dream. Unfortunately, no one knows for sure what Mary's grandfather's dream was for his business relative to the family.

A well-designed education plan can also provide resources for family members unfamiliar with the language of business, such as a small business-related library, or tuition to take classes or seek a degree in business.

Another component of an education plan could be an on-boarding process for younger family members and in-laws. Some families require family members to meet with executives and family members in the business to learn about the business, including its performance, strategy, and plans for the future. This requirement would yield an understanding of how the economic decisions within the business personally affect family members, whether they are present and future owners or non-owning family members whose lives are touched by the business.

A well-designed education plan helps family members understand how their needs and the needs of the business interact and affect each other. A lack of sensitivity to this interplay of family and business has destroyed many families and many businesses. Educating family members can be an opportunity to perpetuate the legacy of the family in pursuit of what matters most to them while creating wealth through the growth of the business.

---

**Jenny's Perspective: Introducing Spouses**

By including new spouses in family meetings, you are welcoming them into the family system, explaining what it is they're now part of. Like it or not, they are there, and by including them you're positioning the family to move forward in a positive manner. The benefit for the in-laws is that they can gather their own data and form their own opinions, rather than hearing the events of the meeting through the filter of their spouses.

We have seen the alternate version of this scenario: The family recognizes only blood relatives in the decision-making body, such as the family meeting or family council. In our experience, this approach breeds resentment and mistrust, which has the power to wreak havoc with the family and eventually with its legacy.

By including spouses as equals, the family is recognizing them as an important and welcome addition. Many of our clients create a ritual to take place at new in-laws' first official family function, such as the annual family meeting: a formal welcome by the family council leader; a ceremonial handshake; the addition of their own branch to the family tree diagram; or some other creative way of saying "We're glad you're here."

Including spouses

- Empowers them to react favorably to the group
- Provides the opportunity for them to form their own opinions without the filter of their spouse
- Allows them to observe their spouse in action in family business matters
- Enables them to add their own talents to the family council (perhaps they are skilled at photography and could begin to document family gatherings)
- Promotes fresh ideas and different points of view
- Creates an atmosphere of positivity

We also encourage the family to consider creating a document for new spouses that provides information on family history, the family enterprise, and the family's governance structures.

**Model Orientation Process for New Family Members**

As spouses and adult children who have reached adulthood are added to the family, and before they attend an annual family meeting, the following three steps are taken:

1. Each new member meets with the leader of their family's branch, in order to get a general overview of the family vision, mission, and charter.
2. Each new member is introduced to the family enterprise by the family business leaders. New members are required to:
   - Take a tour of the family business.
   - Learn the history and current structure of the company.
   - Understand what the company makes or does.
   - Understand the current business climate.

- Learn about leadership's plans for the future.
- Understand the family's interaction with the business via the family council and the board of advisors/directors.

3. Each new member meets with their family branch representative who is on the family council to learn about the family governance plan, including:
   - Continuity: The family story, family mission statement, and family vision statement.
   - Governance: The structures, systems, processes, and strategies used in making purpose-driven family decisions.
   - Succession: How the family is thinking about and handling ownership and management transitions and how the family is positioning and preparing new family members for their roles and responsibilities associated with the family's enterprise.

**What Might Have Been**

What if I'd been educated about business in general and Mary's family's business in particular? Some of this is Economics 101.

*Lesson #1: Save.* Mary's dad set up her savings account so she'd be able to use it just as we did in making the down payment on our house. We learned through her father's efforts that setting something aside for future needs is wise.

*Lesson #2: Save and invest.* This is a corollary to lesson #1. To replenish and/or grow your savings and investments, don't spend everything you make, including distributions from a family business. Annually placing some of your savings in investments magnifies your wealth.

*Lesson #3: Look ahead.* Given my limited understanding of what was happening in the family business I naturally thought that all of Mary's share of the profits should be paid out to her. I eventually convinced Mary to sell her interest in her family's business, which I regret. The wealth-creating opportunities she lost by selling were enormous. If the family business is to be a legacy asset for multiple generations, then it has to grow, creating new wealth for an ever larger family.

The law of populations states that as a population grows, it will eventually consume the resources available to it. Resources need to grow faster than the population it feeds or the population will die.

Hence the wealth-creating role of a family business. Grow the business if you want to provide for future generations.

How families view this objective determines where and how legacy wealth needs to grow. If a family deems its business the wealth-creating engine for the family, enough profit needs to be retained to fuel this growth. Profits available for distribution beyond what is needed for sustainable growth can then be used by family members in their pursuit of what matters most to them.

Families who own businesses will always need to decide how best to leverage them. Do you constantly reinvest profit to expand the business or do you distribute all profits to the owners? Many family businesses try to find a middle ground, using a portion of the profits to expand and a portion to make distributions.

The good news for Mary's family is that I didn't harm or destroy the family or the business. Both are flourishing. The fifth generation of eventual family business owners has arrived, and we are still together! We have defied the odds—most family-owned businesses don't survive past the third generation.

I've used the lessons I've learned as the spouse of a third-generation family business owner to help other families avoid our mistakes. In my role as a second-generation business owner in my own family, I've used the knowledge I've gained from my experiences with Mary's family to help formulate the Casellas' governance and succession plans.

### What This Means For You

No family is immune from the mistakes I made. The ones who are thoughtful and purposeful about helping everyone in the family to be fulfilled, happy, and together and are willing to do the hard work to overcome the challenges of being in business together are the ones who thrive.

Ignorance and secrecy are dangerous conditions within families who own an enterprise that is intended to be passed down through generations. Research shows that less than 1 in 3 families transition their enterprise from the 1st to the 2nd generation. Fewer than 1 in 9 survive into the 3rd generation. To overcome these odds, families who take the time to educate family members to be positioned and prepared to handle the responsibilities that are to come will greatly enhance the probability of successfully transitioning from one generation to the next.

Are you preparing your children and grandchildren for their future roles within the family and the enterprise?

/ 11 /

# Using Success Mapping to Manage Change

How do you think about the future? Do you anticipate what the future might be? Do you make plans and take action before change actually occurs? Or do you wait for circumstances to dictate how you respond or act?

Change happens. Whether it is expected or comes as a surprise, change confronts all of us throughout our lives. We may not be able to directly or even indirectly influence it or its outcome, but how we choose to respond to change is totally within our control.

Addressing an anticipated change under calm conditions, before it becomes a crisis, is always desirable. You are at a far greater risk of a bad outcome when you're forced to deal with change on the fly.

Whether you take the initiative to plan for potential change issues before they occur or you react to a change underway, using a change management process such as success mapping will greatly enhance your chances of reaching a favorable outcome.

## Reactive vs. Proactive

The difference between proactively dealing with change and reactively addressing change is very simple. Timing. Both approaches respond to change. The question for you is when do you choose to respond? Before, during, after, or never?

When life is good, why would a family want to think about problems that haven't yet appeared on the horizon? It seems like borrowing trouble. Nonetheless, change will occur.

Avoiding change is a primal trait that has been hard-wired into each of us since the dawn of time. We as a species prefer to be safe. The unknown may pose a threat. So a family's natural tendency is to let sleeping dogs lie rather than risk stirring up any trouble by anticipating an important change.

The primal response is reactive: fight or flight. The more evolved mind-set is to proactively manage change by channeling your energy in a way that allows you to see the big picture and plan accordingly.

If you and your family recognize the need to proactively address change, you may avoid being distracted by the emotionality associated with it when it occurs. If, however, you need to react to an unexpected change as it is occurring, you may also have to manage the emotions that are aroused. Dealing with these emotions is an extra layer of work.

In either case, once change is being addressed, success mapping can provide the process to best manage it, enabling you to focus on the change through the perspective of your life experiences. As a change management process, success mapping builds on each step of your journey—past, present, and future. Gaining an understanding of your journey lets you manage change in a way that reflects your experiences and expectations. Success mapping gives you the structure for getting to know who you are today and what matters most to you. Managing change using this framework will most likely lead to a better outcome. You will be able to move beyond the volatility of a fight-or-flight reaction and engage the higher-functioning parts of your brain to think the issues through, guided by the principles that reflect your journey.

A word of caution here for families facing significant change: Don't try to manage the process on your own. An experienced professional who is trained in change management can help you navigate the process, especially in an emotionally charged environment. An outside facilitator/mediator can serve as an intermediary should a discussion become contentious between family members.

### Keys to Managing Change

To successfully manage change within families, four key elements need to be in place:

- *Shared values.* What do we stand for as a family? How can we use those values and beliefs to make important decisions on issues that affect our family?
- *Foresight.* How do we manage the ownership and leadership transitions that lie ahead? What do we need to learn?
- *Effective communication.* How do we interact with one another? Are we able to hear what is being said? Do we respect each other's point of view?
- *Conflict resolution.* When we have a disagreement, are we able to work it out?

The first two elements, knowing what you stand for and where you want to go, are covered in earlier chapters. Let's take a closer look at these last two elements.

### Managing Change through Effective Communication

Communication is the ability to share ideas, listen, and be heard that leads to a mutual understanding of each others' views.

What if one of your children wanted to talk to you about her interest in being more involved in the family business? Would you be willing to talk? Would you be willing to listen? What if her interest didn't fit in with your plans for her future? Would your child feel safe talking to you?

The key to resolving such an issue is the quality of your relationship with your child. Healthy family relationships are built on the foundation of effective communication. Does your family communicate effectively enough to manage significant change?

---

**Jenny's View: Keys to Effective Communication**

The word *communication* comes up so often in our work. It is the villain in family dysfunction and the hero in family cohesiveness. When people have made the effort to figure out how they can effectively talk and, more important, listen to each other, they are more likely to be able to withstand change and conflict and to prosper through time.

Communication is the crucial ingredient in maintaining and nurturing relationships inside or outside the family.

Families we see who have remained intact past the third generation have taken the time to figure this communication thing out. They have recognized that it's the primary factor in being able to remain a family, a business, a foundation, or whatever else they want to be.

Members of these successful families have all made the commitment to listen, to understand, and to consider each other's points of view. This is the start. Once a family has the willingness and awareness to work on how they talk, but mostly listen, to each other, there is the basis for healthy agreement and disagreement.

Along with this commitment to listen, there must also be a safe atmosphere for people to express themselves. For example, many families make a point of having dinner together. The table becomes the place to tell each other their thoughts and feelings. This is just one way parents can create a space for their children to share what's on their minds. Once kids feel they're being listened to, they also feel respected, which can lead to a level of self-confidence that will serve them well when they're on their own.

This safe place for listening and talking becomes more essential as family members grow, mature, and begin to form opinions and behaviors that might not match their immediate family's patterns. Think of the teenage years, when family norms are naturally tested as a child explores how he fits in outside the family bubble. The open communication link becomes vital as a lifeline for the teen to know he is still and always connected to people who care and support him.

Families who have fostered open communication can draw on their comfort with each other as they face changes. Some of these changes are a result of the natural progression of time, such as graduating from school. Some changes will be more abrupt, such as a death or divorce.

When families have committed to making communication a priority and provide a safe place for it to happen, they will eventually develop a "core" that gives them an advantage when conflict, change, and crises come knocking. Families who have learned that the family is a source of strength and can withstand adversity are less likely to dissolve in a sea of emotions and reactivity.

Families who struggle with talking, listening, and relating to each other have no "core" to rely on when times get tough. The members are more likely to react emotionally to crisis or change than to handle things in a way that serves each family member well.

**Our Filters**

To truly connect with others and understand their point of view, you have to really hear what they're saying. We all have filters in our brains that process what others say in a way that makes sense to us. The disconnect in communication takes place in the space between when the words leave someone's mouth and when they enter our brain. We all remember the childhood game called Telephone. Playing this game in real life can have undesirable outcomes. You may hear something the other person may not have meant. This happens because you are using your filter, which can be influenced by:

- Past experiences: Has this person been truthful with you in the past?
- Cultural references: Are you used to hearing these words and phrases?
- Current physical state: Are you tired, hungry, thirsty?
- Current emotional state: Are you angry or sad about something unrelated?

All of these factors can combine to color what has been said. We don't decide to run everything past our filter; it happens automatically.

Understanding that everyone goes through this process is a first step in establishing authentic communication. Really listening and confirming that what you heard is what the other person meant is vital, especially in times of conflict or stress.

Through the years, we have developed a few rules that we pass out at an initial family meeting. Once the participants have all read them, we ask for a commitment to abide by them. We warn them that these rules are harder to follow than they seem on paper, but if they succeed over time, they will notice a definite improvement in how they communicate and generally get along with each other.

**Rules for Improving Communication**

- Make time to meet one to one. The effort it takes to do this indicates you think the other person is a priority.
- Make eye contact. When you talk and, more important, when you listen, looking into the other person's eyes signals your full engagement in what she is saying. If someone is speaking to you and you're looking over her shoulder or around the room, she will notice that you're not actually listening.
- Don't interrupt. There is a reason we have two ears and one mouth. Listen. You will have your chance to speak. This encourages respect.

- Don't raise your voice. This rule seems self-evident if you are truly trying to communicate; however, things can go off the rails of good intention quickly. If this rule is in place and agreed to, the conversation can remain on track. If a conversation becomes heated, we intervene and ask the parties to stop talking altogether. We identify what seems to be the issue at hand, and ask whether all agree. We then resume the conversation with different rules so that the issue is being attacked, not the person.

  Each person addresses us with his opinion while the other party listens without interrupting. The other party is then asked to summarize what she has just heard. This forces each one to acknowledge the other, not necessarily agreeing with but respecting what is being said. This usually defuses the emotionality that can take over in a heated conflict. Once we have gone through this process, giving both participants the opportunity to express their thoughts, we agree to at least one or two points of common ground. That is where we restart the conversation.
- Don't talk about or on behalf of someone else. This is a big one. This is the one that takes the most practice. By not talking about others, you have put your emphasis on the person you are talking *with*. This rule also eliminates gossip and hearsay. Those two things have a lot of power. They usually serve to advance someone else's agenda, not yours. Let others fight their own battles. By sticking to what you want out of this time you are spending with this person, you have a better chance of achieving a higher level of communication, trust, and respect. This approach also encourages others to address their issues with the person they have the issue with instead of deflecting that negative energy onto you. By not allowing yourself to be "triangled" into someone else's drama, you are establishing yourself as someone who will not tolerate or encourage negativity.
- Use "I," not "You." When someone leads with "You," the tone can sometimes become accusatory and in some cases downright hostile. If, instead, "I" is used, the listener will be more open to what comes next. It also causes the speaker to be careful about what he is saying, because he is owning it.
- Don't talk about the weather. Avoid topics that are too general, such as the weather or the local sports team. You have taken the time to meet—make it count. Learn something new about the other person each time you see her. You'll be surprised how

much you can learn from someone if you ask something like what she hopes to accomplish today or what was the favorite thing he did this week. Seen any movies or gone to any good restaurants lately? You can always find something interesting about someone if you ask what her interests are. Each time gets easier as you establish a rapport that extends beyond the surface of your everyday interactions.

### Resolving Conflict Arising From Change

We've all seen stories in the media about business-owning families in conflict. Most of them end badly. Take for example the Pritzker family. Jay Pritzker, the founder of Hyatt Hotels, amassed a fortune estimated at $30 billion. He wanted to preserve the Pritzker legacy for many generations by keeping the companies intact. Unfortunately, this would not be the case.

Following his death in 1999, two of his grandchildren sued their father alleging he misappropriated funds from a family trust. The lawsuit was settled with each of the grandchildren receiving about $450 million.

Then other family members accused family leaders of mishandling business transactions. The family's empire has since been divided up between other family members. Jay Pritzker's dream of preserving the family legacy is no longer a possibility.

Who's right? Who's wrong? Who will win? Resolving differences starts with finding common ground.

Family members should identify aspects of the business that they see eye to eye on. This might be a shared belief about why the business exists in the first place. Or it might be a shared vision of what they want the company to look like in the future. Then the conversation can shift to the matter at hand, framed within the bigger picture of what matters most to them.

Let's take a look at how the success mapping process helped two families manage an important change. The first story shows what happened to a family when they incorporated the success mapping process to work their way through a sudden and unexpected change. The second family provides a great illustration of the power of proactively planning for change.

**Death of a Legacy**

When Fred died three months after being diagnosed with cancer at 72, his wife Leanne and their two sons were not prepared for what happened next.

Fred and his cousin Ron co-owned the family business. Their fathers had started their logistics company many years ago. Upon their retirement Fred, who had just turned 55, was appointed to lead the company. He inherited his father's 50 percent share of the business, and Ron likewise inherited his own father's 50 percent following his death.

Ron was never happy about the succession decision that his father signed off on. He believed it showed his father didn't think he was good enough to lead the business. He also didn't like having Fred's sons working in the business—he knew they were being groomed to succeed Fred who was planning to retire when he turned 75. Ron was convinced he would never get the chance to run the business.

When Fred died Ron appointed himself president without any objection from Fred's wife, Leanne. He interpreted this as his opportunity to gain total control and ownership of the company. He approached Leanne and insisted that she sell her interest in the business to him immediately. He implied that this would be the only way she would ever see any real money come to her and her family from the business.

Leanne had no interest in running the business and Fred had not told her that he was planning to appoint their sons as his successor when he retired. It did not occur to her to talk to the boys about their interest in the business. Not knowing Fred's plan, she decided that she would sell her husband's interest to Ron.

Leanne sold her shares at a price that was based on a formula in the operating agreement intended to discourage anyone from selling their interest. It was 40 percent less than its appraised value. The formula did not include a provision for selling an interest of a deceased owner at the appraised price rather than the discounted price she received. All Leanne knew was that she needed the money from the business to maintain her lifestyle.

Upon hearing the news that Leanne had sold Fred's interest in the business her sons were very upset. They quickly realized their uncle had taken advantage of their mother. They believed he kept his conversations with their mother a secret from them because he didn't want them to be his business partners.

The boys knew their father wanted them to succeed him in running the business someday. He saw it as a way of keeping the boys together. But, the operating agreement hadn't been updated since it was originally drafted many years ago. No one imagined then that the business might be something for the 3rd generation of the family to consider. Nothing in the document gave guidance on transferring interests to next-generation family members.

Now Fred was gone and so was his share of the business. This put Fred's family at a cross-roads. What would keep Leanne and her sons together now? Would the sale of the business be the end of the family? Everyone could go their own way. Or they could attempt to make the most of their circumstances to produce a more appealing outcome.

Fred's sons felt strongly about fulfilling their ancestors' dreams of owning and operating a business. They decided they wanted to move forward as a business-owning family. Enter the success mapping process.

Going through the success mapping process, Fred's family was able to articulate and identify exactly what they wanted for themselves and succeeding generations of their family. The family legacy would start anew with Fred's sons.

Fred's sons decided to start a new venture. Leanne agreed to bankroll the venture with the money she received from the sale of Fred's shares. The boys, who enjoyed working with each other, would run the new business using what their father taught them. They narrowed their focus on the areas of the logistics business that provided the greatest opportunity for growth and profits.

Working with their family attorney they devised an ownership structure that gave Leanne more than enough income to allow her to do whatever she wanted. The ownership of the new business was placed in a trust that would further benefit Fred's sons, their children, and future generations.

The family's new business was an overnight success. Sales and profits grew quickly. Within two years, the business was producing far more income than Leanne would have received from the old business. Ron managed to run the old business in the ground and recently filed for bankruptcy.

The dream of owning a family business lived on in this new venture. Leanne lived out her days enjoying her time with her sons and their families. The family legacy survived and thrived because Fred's family managed the sudden, unexpected change using the success mapping process.

**Planning for Change in Leadership**

Joe Tolson founded Tolson Industries 1979. It had grown to a very large international distributor of electrical hardware. Joe wanted to transfer his ownership of the business to his three adult children soon. It was his hope that they would be able to work together in making decisions as the future owners of the business. But, he was concerned that his children were not very close to each other and tended to bicker whenever they were together for family functions.

One of his advisors asked him why it was important for his family to be able to make decisions together. Joe explained that the business represented the bulk of his estate and his dream for the business was that it would benefit each of his kids. Only one of his children was employed in the business, however, Joe's advisor observed that it would be in everyone's interest to prepare for the ownership transition now. Joe's estate plan called for the change in ownership to occur at his death. Joe's advisor encouraged him to consider having the transition take place while Joe was still alive and recommended Coppertree to help him.

We began the success mapping process by asking Joe and his wife Alicia to tell us about their family. Clearly, they were proud of each of their children and talked about their many accomplishments, from their childhood to the present.

We asked Joe and Alicia what their dream was for their children. Not surprisingly, they wanted them to have a good relationship with each other and to enjoy being together. We asked them how that was going presently. Joe frowned and explained that the kids were having some issues. We asked them to explain.

A rift had developed in the past few years between two of their children. Their oldest son had taken over day-to-day operations at

Tolson Industries as the chief operating officer. Their son had worked his way up through the company while he completed an associate's degree in industrial design at the local community college. In his mind, he had a PhD from the School of Hands-On Experience, which he believed was much more valuable than any Ivy League MBA.

The Tolsons' middle child had earned an MBA from a top school before going to work for a highly regarded consulting firm. Although she had never worked for the family business, she was not shy about pointing out best-practice ideas. Their son resented her intrusions, which came in the form of emails she would send him and copy to their father with operational ideas and recommendations for improving performance.

The Tolsons' youngest daughter was literally a world away. She and her husband lived in Dubai with their two young children. He worked for Dubai World as one of the group's lead economists. Their daughter was active in raising their children and enjoying life as an expatriate in one of the most exciting cities in the world. She had no interest in being involved in her father's business, nor did she and her husband need the money.

Just the same, their youngest daughter truly loved being with her parents and siblings. She cherished the time they were able to be together and wanted nothing to get in the way of everyone coming together to celebrate holidays, traditions, and special family events. She was aware that her older brother and sister were quarreling about the business and she wished they could resolve their differences.

We asked Joe to talk a little bit more about his dream for his family to benefit from the wealth he had created through his business. He explained that the future for the business was bright, and he believed that if his estate and succession plan were structured to allow continued ownership of the business by the family, everyone would benefit.

We then focused our time on identifying what the possibilities were for the Tolsons going forward. Everyone agreed that staying together was a very important goal.

Their son and older daughter wanted to be together as a family as long as they could resolve their differences pertaining to the business. As we talked with Joe and Alicia more about the issue of business leadership, we learned that their son wanted to be recognized for his contribution to the success of the business. Their daughter wanted to share ideas with the management of Tolson Industries from what she had learned through her educational and consulting experiences.

In the course of the conversations that take place throughout the success mapping process, family members find themselves learning about each other as they listen to everyone's stories and comments. This was the case for the two older Tolson children. As they listened to each other they saw that they both wanted the same thing: to help make the business more and more successful. They realized they each had unique skills and abilities that could be used in different ways to achieve that goal.

Their daughter realized that her brother's relationship with the workforce was invaluable in cultivating a culture of quality and pride in exceeding customer expectations. Listening to his sister talk about what she was able to do for her clients, he began to appreciate the value of views and ideas from beyond the four walls of Tolson Industries. He became very interested in learning how businesses his sister worked with in her consulting practice were achieving success. This in turn opened Joe up to the idea of helping his son to gain access to outside advice.

Joe proceeded to put a board of advisors in place and the first person he invited to join it was his older daughter. She was thrilled with the opportunity and vowed to support her brother, whom she saw as the next CEO of the company. Joe agreed and announced shortly thereafter that his son would be taking over as president and CEO by year's end.

Now that their children were no longer at odds, Joe could turn his attention to the transfer of his ownership to his children. What is so powerful to me about this story is that the single issue of managerial transition had the potential to blow this family up.

In choosing to address the managerial succession question before it was forced upon them, the family was able to effect the change in a positive manner. In turn, the bigger change issue of ownership transition could now be addressed in a far less emotional environment.

Change happens and change can be hard. You can manage it now or manage it later. As long as you have a process to manage change you're less likely to suffer the consequences of it managing you.

**Jenny's View: What Does a Well-Functioning Family Do?**

There is no single description of what a well-functioning family looks like. There are common themes, however, that we introduce to the families we serve. Each family has its own variations on these themes. For some, incorporating these techniques means they can have Thanksgiving dinner together without it erupting into a screaming match. For others, it means they are connecting with each other on a deeper level.

Most of the families who seek us out have the desire to achieve their version of success. The challenge is that they are not only navigating the normal ups and downs of family relationships, they are also dealing with those complicated dynamics with their boss/father, co-worker/brother, and manager/cousin. It can get messy.

But the families who have decided they want to be not only a connected family but a successful multigenerational family business have usually taken the time to:

- Share and memorialize their family story with the next generations.
- Articulate the founders' goals for the family and the business (if there is one).
- Share their personal goals with each other.
- Discuss and decide on shared values that lead to defining the family mission or purpose.
- Capture these values and the mission in a document that outlines how the family makes decisions around shared assets in a way that honors their mission.
- Establish a safe place for the family to meet regularly to discuss topics that affect all generations.
- Commit to educating and training the younger generations and include them in all family gatherings.

**The Champion and the Doubter**

Families function well when family members want to be together. Usually there is at least one member we call the champion, who carries the flag of repairing or improving family relationships.

The champion is usually the person who has shone a light on the fact that if the family wants to be one of the few to stay together past the third generation, there is some work to be done.

The champion almost always has a counterpart, the doubter. This is the family member who comes to the meeting with arms crossed, brow furrowed, the "Why are we doing this?" attitude. We have seen this person in every family. We seek them out. Our challenge is to listen to their concerns, address them thoughtfully, and invite them to participate at their own comfort level.

Some doubters seem unmovable, but we've found that once the family has committed to the process of establishing their purpose and wanting to connect, the doubter will eventually look over the fence and join in. Holdouts, however, are not allowed to stop the meeting or the general progress.

We have seen family members attempt to disrupt a meeting and then storm out when it became clear the meeting would go on. We have come to learn that's okay. We acknowledge what has happened, and then move on with the hope that the doubter will rejoin the process when she's ready.

**The Safety Net**

The family is where we learn who we are and how we'll deal with the world once we venture out into it. It is where the capacity to gain self-knowledge and self-confidence is born. At its best, the family structure allows us to risk making mistakes and choices, safe in the knowledge that our parents' love doesn't depend on our doing everything the "right" way or their way.

As a family member or as an individual, how do you interact with others? Are you able to trust that what you are saying is being respected by those who are listening to you? Do you in turn respect what others share with you?

**Managing Conflict**

Conflict happens in all families. It's normal and inevitable. I wouldn't trust someone who says he has never had a disagreement with his family. That unicorn does not exist or is fooling itself.

Conflict is not a dirty word. In fact, it's a natural way to clear the air, gain new perspective, and even deepen relationships. The problem with conflict is that many times, it isn't acknowledged, which allows it to fester, gather strength, and reappear, usually in times of family stress. It becomes the elephant in the room.

**Become an Elephant Trainer**

Invite the elephant in. Ignoring him gives him more power. Acknowledging him forces everyone to talk. In our experience, the mere act of identifying what the issue is goes a long way in defusing it. In many cases, especially in multigenerational families, there may be cousins who aren't talking to each other and they don't even know why.

Addressing a conflict with a family member is hard. It's uncomfortable. It's easier to leave it alone, but that's when it does the most damage.

We usually begin with saying, "We're noticing some tension; let's discuss it in a way that moves you forward." This is where the Rules of Communication on page 129 are used.

Identify the facts of the issue, then identify the emotions of the issue. Separating these two forces allows both parties to see that emotion may be clouding each other's perspective.

Talking about the conflict in a nonthreatening manner is especially important. Many see the family meeting as a safe place to address conflicts. Having a skilled facilitator on hand is key in successfully airing and resolving conflicts.

A skilled facilitator will also help the parties understand that each person has a role/responsibility in the conflict. It didn't arise in a vacuum. Accepting that can lead to defusing the situation and discussing the possibility of common ground. Once the common ground is established, there is a path to understanding.

## What This Means For You

Dealing with change can be very hard. Nonetheless we all face change throughout our lives. Within the context of families who co-own an enterprise or shared asset, having a plan and a process to manage change can minimize the potential damage of an improperly addressed change issue.

/ PART FIVE /

# Achieving Success

/ 12 /

# Executing the Legacy Strategy

## ROLE OF ADVISORS

Now that you have created your legacy strategy, what will it take to achieve your goals and dreams?

The beauty of the success mapping process is its ability to help you assemble and direct the necessary resources and expertise needed to achieve your measures of success. Expertise in this case refers to your legal advisors, your tax and accounting advisors, your banking advisors, your financial advisors, your risk managers, a family office, and anyone else needed to help you in living your legacy. Whether you direct your advisors or you rely on the advisor you most trust to manage what needs to be done, the execution of your legacy strategy requires the expertise from multiple disciplines.

In chapter 8 the Winston family's life capital framework was transformed into a legacy strategy. An excerpt of their strategy was presented on pp. 95–99. The excerpt of the strategy identified four objectives the family intended to pursue in the coming year. Let's look at what it would take, in terms of expertise, to achieve each of them.

***Objective # 1: Family Distributions***

Expertise needed:

- CEO—Establish the business plan to support the family's objective of receiving a $1.2 million after-tax distribution

- Board of Directors—Review and approve business plan and special distribution plan
- Company CFO—Review and assess the company's historic results, forecast for the current fiscal year, and monitor financial performance and cash flow throughout the year
- Banker—Work with the CFO to evaluate the most attractive financing plan using the line of credit, cash reserves on the company's books, cash flow, or a combination of these funding vehicles
- Each household's financial advisors—Best use of distributions once received; spend, save, or invest
- Company president—Present the profit-sharing bonuses with each of the employees at the next quarterly meeting.

***Objective # 2: Growth and Income Plan for the Family LLC***

Expertise needed:

- Financial advisors—Review current investment strategy and evaluate the proposed goals-based investment strategy to determine the best course of action in meeting the family's spending policy of 3% per year
- Investment consultant—Search, due diligence and recommendations of appropriate investment managers to use in agreed upon strategy
- Tax advisor—Review tax liabilities of proposed changes to investment policy

***Objective # 3: Giving Strategy for Winston Family Foundation***

Expertise needed:

- Foundation board—Review present grant recipients and conduct search for new grantees for 2016 giving plan
- Family Council—Review board's recommendations and select grantees for coming year

***Objective # 4: Family Stewardship Program***

Expertise needed:

- Family legacy consultant—Develop a next generation education curriculum for 3rd generation family members

- Family legacy committee—Work with legacy consultant to plan stewardship sessions at family meeting
- Financial advisor—Work with family council to develop a financial literacy education program for next year's family meeting

The advisors listed above are but a few the Winston family would be working with throughout the year to achieve these and many more measures of what they identified as the life they wish to experience.

Managing the complexity and breadth of what needs to be done borders on being a full-time job for legacy asset-owning families. Most families will choose to outsource the management of this process to their most trusted advisor. With the legacy strategy as a framework for pursuing success, whether it is a family member or trusted advisor, the family's potential for pursuing what matters most will enhance the likelihood of meaningfully living a legacy that lasts.

---

**Coppertree's Perspective: Family Meeting Guide for Advisors**

*Pre-Meeting*

- **Meet with all participants.**
  By doing this, you are taking the time to hear what is on everyone's mind. These are the topics that will populate the agenda. This is also the time to listen for possible "elephants"—topics that can derail an unprepared facilitator. Understanding what these issues are will allow you to put them in their place during the meeting. In other words, the elephant can be invited in, but he cannot take over the meeting.
- **Provide an agenda.**
  Allowing the participants to add to, comment on, or question the topics before the meeting starts can save time and awkwardness during it. Be willing to adjust the agenda to adequately reflect the family's needs. It is important for the family to see this as their meeting, not yours.
- **Assign a role in the meeting to as many family members as possible.**
  Doing this drives home the fact that this is their meeting. This is their opportunity to establish their unique family identity. It also instills a sense of pride in the members who are taking charge of their portion of the meeting. For example, as the facilitator, you would ask a G-2 (a member of the second generation of busi-

ness owners) to present the family tree to the group. Another task would be to have a family member begin the meeting with a family story, (we do this on a rotating basis so all family members eventually have a turn). When you have three or four members actually presenting at the meeting, the excitement level is dramatically increased. Instead of expecting to be lectured to, participants become involved and engaged.

- **Visit the meeting location ahead of time if possible.** Nothing kills attendees' attention quicker than a room that is too hot, too cold, or too small. Also, by scoping out the location you can head off any other ambushes. The last thing you want to deal with on meeting day is the absence of handicapped ramps for Grandpa or an indoor hotel pool for little Joey. Secure the family's audiovisual, wi-fi, transportation, and meal/snack needs well ahead of time.
- **Assign a family member to take and distribute meeting notes.** Having notes from previous meetings can resolve differing memories of a particular discussion or decision. It also feeds into the idea of having family members responsible for portions of their meeting. This can be done on a rotating basis.

### *Meeting Day*

- Assign a family member to meet and greet members as they arrive.
- Have the G-1 hosts open the meeting declaring their hope for the day.
- Use an icebreaker exercise to loosen everyone up and establish an atmosphere of informality and inclusiveness.
- As the facilitator, take the time to confirm everyone's commitment to a productive meeting.
- Be flexible; the family may want to explore a topic beyond the allotted time. Let that happen and move other topics to the next meeting.
- Take breaks every hour and a half.
- Use exercises and demonstrations as much as you can to illustrate points and to make the meeting interactive.
- Have each person talk about his best takeaway from the meeting.
- Have the G-1 or meeting host close the meeting with her thoughts.
- Set a date for the next meeting.

**If the elephant tries to take control:**

Family meetings are fertile ground for sensitive subjects. We have witnessed meetings where the facilitators were blindsided by the introduction of such subjects and subsequently lost all control of the meeting and any hope of assisting the family with their goals. This possibility reinforces the importance of meeting with all parties ahead of time and being aware of issues the family is facing. When a sensitive subject is broached, acknowledge that it should be addressed because ignoring it isn't healthy. In discussing it, however, be clear that you will be leading and monitoring the discussion so that it moves forward in a positive way. We use this method when facing highly emotional topics in a family meeting:

- Give each person a chance to speak to the issue, addressing the facilitator.
- Use "I" instead of "You."
- Don't allow interruptions; give each person a turn.
- Repeat what you, the facilitator, thought was said and ask for the speaker's acknowledgment.
- Have the speaker do the same.
- Ask each person what he learned.

Afterward, the emotional content has been defused and the participants may be ready to understand each other enough to agree to be open to further discussion. Don't expect them to always agree or to "hug it out"; the best you can hope for is that they feel heard and understand each other's point of view.

***Post-Meeting***

After the meeting, remember to follow up with each individual. In these follow-up calls, you will receive valuable information for the next meeting. Touch base with the family note taker and offer help and advice if needed. There may have been some action items that require attention from other family members. Connect with those people who have volunteered their time to do something for the family and offer advice and assistance.

The success mapping process has been life-changing for the families we serve at Coppertree. Most all of our families have shared how this new approach to planning for the future has opened their minds and their hearts to what really matters.

The success mapping process can be used by anyone. The process provides a straightforward means to use what you have to pursue what you want based on what is important to you. It puts purpose to the vision to provide direction on how best to use the resources you have at your disposal.

What does this mean to you? It puts you in control of what you need to do or have done. As an example, what if your tax advisor contacts you and recommends a strategy that would derive significant tax benefits for you? Would it be beneficial for you to follow the advisor's recommendation?

Within the context of all else that may be occurring in your life at the time of the recommendation, such a move may be more detrimental than helpful. What if the advisor's idea required most of the cash you have available to take advantage of the strategy while at the same time you are planning for your daughter's wedding? Which is more important?

This is not to say that a tax saving strategy is a bad idea. But you must be able to make resource allocation decisions fully aware of all that is important to you. The success mapping process gives you and your advisors the full picture of what you need and want based on what is important to you. Tax savings and funding weddings are both important.

Taken together in a balanced approach, you can make the best decisions for you and your family in how you choose to allocate your resources in pursuit of what matters most.

**What This Means For You**

Rarely, will a family be able to create, implement, and execute the success mapping process on their own. Most families over their lifetime have been able to surround themselves with trusted advisors who are capable, competent, and valuable. Using your team of expert advisors in your pursuit of what matters most as you live your legacy will allow you to focus on what is important to you.

The success mapping process can do wondrous works for your family. Whether you pursue it on your own or through the assistance of your advisors, you can achieve your dream of living a legacy that lasts.